The Glider

by Linda Summerford

Dedication

My sweet sister, Wanda
my loving sister, Martha,
my wonderful, encouraging husband, Richard,
my beautiful, precious daughters, Jeni and Lisa,
my handsome grandsons, Leland, Aydin, and Averi,
my adorable granddaughters, Rilyn and Emerson
All of my loving, accepting, and caring aunts,
uncles, and cousins,
may we treasure our memories and leave a legacy
of which we can be proud.

To all the children who are living in foster care
and to those who are adopted,
may you always know you are truly loved.

Endorsements

The Glider tells a story - Linda's story - of the beauty that can come from brokenness. While not shying away from the life-long effects trauma, foster care, a flawed child welfare system, and even adoption can have on a child, she illustrates the life-changing potential of adoption to heal and allow a child to move beyond the brokenness. Ultimately, her story is a powerful reminder of each of our own stories of redemption - where God calls us from the sinful brokenness we were born into to a place of healing through his salvation and grace.

~Holly Gillespie Pisarik, attorney

In this day and age, child abuse is rampant. The news and social media fill our heads with tragic events, and seldom do we hear about the ones with a positive ending. But, in The Glider, Linda Summerford—with transparency and a heart of love and forgiveness—shares her own poignant story of redemption and healing from a childhood filled with abuse. The Glider is a testimony to God's mercy, protection, and goodness. It is a story that will stay with you forever. Grab a tissue when you read this book.

~Andrea Merrell, author and editor

Linda's story caught my heart from the beginning and never let go. Powerful, inspiring and filled with hope despite the terrifying darkness she and her three siblings had to endure, her story shows how authentic love truly can conquer all.

~Jessica Brodie, author

Heart wrenching reality in a captivating read. The unspoken truths of a system trusted to protect our children. Linda Summerford's vulnerability reveals details so hard to believe, but those of us in the system see it regularly. If the years had not been printed, this could be present day in so many ways. May Linda's story bring about the change so desperately needed in foster care.

~Ali Bragdon, founder and CEO of Oasis of Hope Ministries

The Glider shines light into dark places, revealing truths concerning the foster care system. Linda's personal testimony, though painful, points to the redemptive nature of a Savior who promises to bring beauty from brokenness and never wastes a suffering. This true story won't merely touch readers' hearts, it inspires us to prayerfully consider what difference we might make in the lives of children.

~Maureen Miller, author

Though our stories are different, mine and Linda's have a few things in common. The best parts being we were both adopted by wonderful Christian parents, and we both have served on the Governor's Taskforce to reform the Foster Care and Adoption services in South Carolina. The children trapped in a cycle of abuse because of a broken system is just as heart-wrenching and unacceptable today as it was when Linda and Wanda were adopted. My hope and prayer is that through Linda's beautiful story of love and redemption, more children will be rescued from perpetual abuse and find their loving, forever families—sooner rather than later.

~ Melanie Shull, author, publisher, and editor

Linda Summerford paints a painful and poignant story made even stronger by the fact that it is her story—real, raw, and redemptive. It spotlights the dangers of a broken system and extends the hope that one person—or maybe two—can change a child's life forever.
~Lori Hatcher, author

Adoption Creed

Not flesh of my flesh,
Nor bone of my bone,
But still miraculously
My own.
Never forget
For a single minute
You did not grow under my heart,

But in it.

by Fleur Conkling

The Glider

A True Story of Survival
From Heartbreak to Hope

Linda Summerford

Abundance
Books

The Glider: a True Story of Survival from Heartbreak to Hope
Written by Linda H. Summerford

ISBN: 979-8-9880360-0-5 (print)
ISBN: 979-8-9880360-7-4 (ePub)

Abundance Books
417 Forest St, #445
Kalamazoo, MI 49001

Disclaimer

The names of the sisters, adoptive parents, and other relatives throughout this book are accurate. For security and identification purposes, the names of the biological mother and father have been changed.

This story is a work of creative nonfiction, based on a true story. Some of the characters and events are the product of the author's childhood memories, testimonies of others, and research. Some of the content in this book is a crafted account based on interviews and information obtained from records from the South Carolina Department of Social Services and other research.

Characters resembling any living or deceased person, other than those stated as based on historical characters, is coincidental.

Acknowledgments

Richard Summerford, my sweetheart for more than fifty years. You always believed in me and persuaded me to write my story for the sake of the children.

Lisa Roes, my baby girl. You bring my words to life. Thank you for all the hours you sacrificed toiling over my manuscript, bringing the scenes alive, and giving voice to each character. God has blessed you with much creativity, both in designing wedding gowns and in art. I believe He has great plans for your future as you trust and follow His leading. You are an example of true beauty to your children. Thank you for the joy you have brought into my life.

Jeni Summerford, my firstborn daughter. Thank you for your faith in me and your positive comments as I shared ideas with you.

Aunts, Uncles, and Cousins, thank you to all my wonderful family for not giving up on me in my endeavor to write about our great family. Each time I shared a chapter at the Christmas family reunion, all of you were wiping your tears and hugging me. Your encouragement means the world to me. I hope the words I have penned here do justice to the legacy my parents left for us all. You can certainly be proud of the Elmore and Haney family names.

Martha and Wanda, my beloved sisters. The phrase what Satan meant for evil, God used for good is so true in our lives. I am grateful every day that God reunited us. Thank you for being the best sisters. You blessed my life. May God use our story to uplift others and bring about much-needed changes in the system so the next generation won't suffer as we did.

Brenda Roberts, I don't know where to begin, my dear friend. Thank you for all you've meant to my family. You cared for our sweet mother during the last years of her life. I can never thank you enough for the sacrifices you made. She loved it when you called her "Miss Lydia." You were like another daughter. God could not have chosen a better caregiver than you for our wonderful mother. There will be stars in your crown for sure.

Holly Pisarik, Attorney, Pisarik Law Firm, Fort Mill, SC. Former Director, SC Department of Labor, Licensing and Regulation; General Counsel to former Governor, Nikki Haley. I was honored to be ask to be your assistant at LLR those many years ago. We became more than boss and employee as our friendship grew. Thank you for always taking time to listen to my ideas and thoughts about writing. You led by example. Your belief in my success has now carried me through to a finished book. I will be forever grateful.

Christa T. Bell, Attorney, Sumter County Solicitor's Office, Sumter, SC. It's always good if you can be friends as well as coworkers. That's how is was for us. We worked together over twelve years at LLR and I looked forward to coming to work each day. You have always shared with me your writing tips. Many things I learned from proper legal writing I have been able to use in writing books. Professionalism was always top priority and you taught me so much about always putting my best work on paper. We loved each others families and have stayed close through all these years. Thank you for your many kindnesses shown to me.

Melanie Shull, author and mentor, founder and editor-in-chief, Living Real Magazine, author of Unlocked Hearts, Unleased Joy-Forgiveness is Key. Thank you, Melanie for being such an encouraging mentor. I am so glad I met you at the Word Weavers of Lexington, SC, writers group. I can never thank you enough for your encouragement to me as you kept telling me to never give up on my dream of becoming a published author. You prayed with me. You met with me anytime

I asked. You showed me that my story would change people's lives and would be used by God to touch others. I am forever in your debt.

Lori Hatcher, leader of Word Weavers, Lexington, SC, author of Refresh Your Faith: Uncommon Devotions from Every Book of the Bible and Hungry for God...Starving for Time: Five Minute Devotions for Busy Women. Winner of the Christian Small Publisher 2016 Book of the Year. Thank you, Lori, for welcoming me to Word Weavers of Lexington. Sometimes I wish I had joined a lot sooner, but I know God's timing is perfect. It is through Word Weavers that I gained confidence to continue on with writing my story as members of the group meticulously and kindly critiqued each chapter. Thank you for your patience and advice as I struggled to put pen to paper and follow my dream of becoming a published author.

Jean Wilund, author, co-president of Lexington (SC) Word Weavers, writer, Revive our Hearts, blogger, speaker, Bible teacher (The Red Thread), and a graduate of Christian Communicators. You, too, were there with me along the way as I gained confidence in my writing each month at the Word Weavers meeting. I couldn't take notes fast enough as you gave instruction on writing tips. God has truly blessed you with the gift of teaching. Thank you for answering God's calling to teach His Word.

I would like to thank all my Word Weavers dear friends and fellow authors who diligently critiqued my work each month. I don't know where I'd be today without the encouragement and support of everyone at Word Weavers of Lexington, SC.

Bethany Jett, author; Platinum Faith: Live Brilliant, Be Resilient & Know Your Worth; They Call Me Mom: 52 Devotions for Every Moment; The Cinderella Rule: A Young Woman's Guide to Happily Ever After; speaker; marketing strategist; ghostwriter; and co-founder of Serious Writer, Inc., and Platinum Literary Services, Inc. I recall the day I nervously stood in line waiting to meet you at the Blue Ridge Christian Writers Conference. My knees were knocking as I listened to successful authors giving advice to the newcomers. I had asked for my first critique of my first chapter. I just knew you were going to say something like "this is nice, but…and I was going to burst into tears. But it was not that way at all. To my great surprise, you said you loved my story, and that I should not give up on completing the manuscript as this is a much-needed platform in society today. I came away from our meeting with new zeal and determination to continue God's call on my life. Thank you for your words of encouragement and your great knowledge in the world of writing.

Andrea Simmons Merrell, associate editor for Christian Devotions Ministries and Lighthouse Publishing of the Carolinas (LPC); professional freelance editor; finalist for the 2016 Editor of the Year Award Blue Ridge Mountains Christian Writers Conference; 2018 Excellence in Writing award by the Christian Editors Network; a graduate of Christian Communicators; finalist in the 2015 USA Best Book Awards; finalist in the 2018 Selah Awards; author of Praying for the Prodigal, Murder of a Manuscript: Writing and Editing Tips to Keep Your Book out of the Editorial Graveyard, and The Gift and Marriage: Make it or Break It. Co-founder of The Write Editing. I first met you at the Blue Ridge Christian Writers Conference. It was my first conference and I was feeling overwhelmed and insecure. You put me at ease right away as you encouraged me to never give up on my story. I'll always remember your willingness to meet me in Spartanburg at a restaurant to go over more edits and ideas for research to fill in the blanks of my memories. Your kindness will never be forgotten.

Jessica Brodie, author, speaker, journalist, blogger, editor, and writing coach; editor of the award-winning South Carolina United

Methodist Advocate, the oldest newspaper in Methodism; owner and operator of a media production and digital marketing agency, Brodie Media. The first time I met you at Word Weavers in Lexington, we hit it off as friends. I got to a point where I felt I needed a coach and an editor to work closely with me to the finish line. You were highly recommended, and I never turned back. You worked diligently with my initial manuscript and gave me constant encouragement to keep going. Your sweet husband, Matt, took over the media part of building my platform, my Facebook page and my author website. Thank you both, dear friends, for being there for me all the way to publication.

Denise Loock, editor, writer, and speaker. As a freelance editor, Denise uses her twenty-nine years of experience as an English teacher to help published and unpublished writers create clean, concise, and compelling manuscripts that will attract acquisition editors and intrigue readers. Thank you, Denise, for your patience with me in editing the proposal and manuscript so that I was able to present the best work possible.

Maureen Miller, wife, mother, and "Mosie," an award-winning author from western North Carolina. She loves to tell about God's goodness and share stories of His extraordinary character, often discovered in ordinary places, and does so as a collaborative author, blogger, and devotion writer. She's a contributing author for Guideposts' "All God's Creatures," as well as Inspire a Fire, Arise Daily, and her local newspaper. Her personal blog is penningpansies.com, and she's currently working on her debut novel. Thank you, Maureen, for your kind words of encouragement to me. You were there with me as we started Word Weavers in Maggie Valley and western North Carolina. Your insight into sharing God's Word as our chaplain is something we all look forward to each month.

Grace Prichard, editor and owner of Whispering Willows Bed & Breakfast, Ridgeway, SC. You have known me since the beginning of my writing career. Thank you for the many hours you spent editing and encouraging me to continue. The days I spent at Whispering Willows Bed & Breakfast were the best and provided me with much needed rest and relaxation at the respite in the woods. God used that time to refresh my zeal to never give up. Thank you for your continued prayers on my behalf.

Michelle Miller, book designer, Miller Multimedia Design Studio. The first time you showed me on the screen just how my book could look as a finished product, I broke down in tears. Thank you for staying up late at night when I couldn't get my one sheet to print correctly. You knew just what to do and never made me feel inadequate.

Eva Marie Everson, president, Word Weavers International. Eva Marie is a CBA bestselling and multiple award-winning author and speaker, including an ECPA Gold Medallion, Christy finalist, a Silver Medallion winner, a Carol, several Maggie and Golden Scroll awards, and an Inspirational Retailers Choice Award. She is one of the original five Word Weavers members, which began in 1997. She served first as the original president (2000-2007) and is now CEO of Word Weavers International, Inc., which serves writers primarily as a national and international group of critique and educational chapters.

You and I met at the Carolina Christian Writers Conference in Spartanburg. I hung on your every word as you critiqued my work. My fifteen minutes was almost up but you said for me to sit still, you had carved out forty-five minutes to talk with me. You and I shared our life stories and even talked about difficulties we had lived through and were still going through. You let me know you were an ordinary woman God was using in extraordinary ways, and He could use me too. Thank you, friend, for your willingness to be used by God to minister to me and so many others through Word Weavers International.

Cortney Donaldson, founder and principal writer at vocem, LLC, and serves as the acquisitions editor with Morgan James Publishing. You and I became fast friends that cold, snowy day at the Carolina Christian Writers Conference in Spartanburg as you smiled at me and told me you loved my story and couldn't wait to read more. Reading your book, Clay Jar Cracked, gave me inspiration to continue writing what was on my heart. Thank you for your many kind words and encouragement to never give up on my dream.

In Memoriam: Carwell and Frances Haney, Mama and Daddy, without whom this book would not be possible. Unable to have children of their own, they gave sacrificially to my sister and me. We were pitiful, little girls of only three and five, lacking in the basics of social graces. They gave tirelessly of their time, patience, and love so that two young sisters could be given a second chance at a normal life. For that, we are forever grateful.

In Memoriam: Virginia Bell, my prayer warrior. You were my prayer warrior daily as you lifted my name up for courage and persistence to write my story. You are gone now, but never forgotten.

In Memoriam: David Jordan, my dear brother. The day we met, I couldn't understand your tears because I had not seen you since I was a baby. Then you told us of the guilt you felt even as a five-year-old boy that you couldn't stop the social workers from taking us. My heart was broken for you. We bonded from that day. I miss you.

In Loving Memory

Frances Olivia Elmore Haney
"My Special Mama"
Carwell Haney
"My Special Daddy"
Elise Elmore
"Grandma"
William David Jordan
"Brother"

I am who I am because you loved me.

Contents

Author's Note

Childhood should be a time for making memories, yet I remember little about my childhood. I believe God erased some memories for my benefit. Despite all the events leading up to that day, my first memory is the day I was adopted. I realize now what a profound day it was in my life.

I hope my story will encourage you to see the positive things in life and strive to overcome the negatives. I also hope to awaken in you an understanding of what foster children experience and how adoption can alter a child's life in a positive way forever.

My younger sister, Wanda, and I were adopted at the ages of three and five, respectively. Before then, we had been in many foster homes and children's homes after we were rescued into state care, her at eight months and me at two years of age. Our brother, David, was the oldest of four children. He was only five when our mother abandoned our family, leaving us children with an alcoholic father. Martha, the second child, was only four. David and Martha were never released for adoption.

The story, as told to us, is that our mother never looked back when she walked out on all four children and went on with her life. She thought she'd signed papers granting permission for all four of her children to be adopted, but our father refused to sign the termination of parental rights paperwork for my two older siblings. Being an alcoholic, he could not care for them, so even though county social workers removed them, they were never released for adoption. They were tossed from one foster home to another, sometimes together, other times separated, and badly abused and neglected in each home. David ran away from his last foster home at age fourteen and lived with our father, caring for him until our father's death in 1990. Martha remained in foster care until she was eighteen, when she "aged out" and married. (The term "aged out" specified that once children turned eighteen, they were no longer a ward of the state and thus could not remain in foster care. The age limit for this term has recently been increased to twenty-one to help prevent homelessness in teenagers no longer supported by the foster care system).

Fortunately, Wanda and I were adopted by a loving Christian family. After more than thirty years of separation, all four children reunited. We determined then to find out what caused our separation.

Foreword

It's Still Happening

"If I hear someone say one more time, 'There's another child who fell through the cracks,' I'm going to scream!" Out of frustration, I bellowed those words during a Foster Care Review Board meeting. I'd been appointed by the governor of South Carolina to serve on the board a little more than a year earlier. In every meeting, someone had said, "It's so sad when there's another child failed by the system."

I barely sleep the night before every meeting I attend as I read the horror stories in the notes. My head hurts. My stomach churns. I have nightmares.

Failed by the system? How can we continue to fail these children? Why do we use this excuse for a child falling through the proverbial cracks? And more than that—why are there still cracks?

One of the criteria to serve on the Foster Care Review Board is being a former foster child. As soon as I learned that, I knew God was calling me to serve. I understand firsthand the feelings these children have and the questions they ask:

What's wrong with me?

Are all these children here because of something they did?

No one wants me.

I'm in their way.

Where's my sister?

I want to go home.

How do I know and understand these feelings? Because my younger sister and I were in foster care for 904 days before we were adopted together. That's two and a half years—almost as long as my sister had been alive. My older siblings, unfortunately, were never released for adoption but were left in foster care until one aged out of the system and the other refused to return to foster care.

Children are not in foster care because they want to be there. They have been traumatized through no fault of their own. While they don't always start out with behavioral problems, many children develop them after being thrown into foster care. Can we blame them? Each child handles trauma differently. They will not tell you they are anxious or scared. They say things like, "My stomach hurts," "My head hurts," or "I feel sick." Some children withdraw and refuse to speak, while others lash out in aggression, although fear, not anger, is what they're feeling.

I was shocked when I recently visited a local children's home. The children lined up like scared lambs as the worker pulled out a plastic container filled with pills. Every single child in that ward was given a pill. I asked the nurse why they were all taking medicine. She quipped, "They all have ADHD, and this is the only way we can control them." I gasped, biting my tongue as my eyes felt like they wanted to bulge out of their sockets. Almost every report I read before the foster care review board meetings has a list of medicines the children are taking. Sure enough, almost every child is on medicine for ADHD—attention-deficit/hyperactivity disorder.

Society and our lawmakers are not meeting the psychological needs of the children in foster care. These children are scared to death when they are removed from their parents, even if they were abused. They have never met the people tasked with caring for them. They don't have an orientation meeting telling them what to expect in foster care like employees have when they get a new job. Children are removed from the only family they know, sometimes in the middle of the night. Then they are forced to sleep in a strange place, many times alone or in a room full of strangers. Many revert to bed-wetting, even though they may not have done that in years. They are traumatized by the actions of their parents, and then they are traumatized again by the system.

There has to be a better way.

Systems don't fail children, people do.

Bound Together

This is the worst case of abuse and neglect I have ever witnessed.

February 23, 1956
Greenville, South Carolina
Trudy Melton, Caseworker

"C'mon, you stupid car!" This was no time for car problems. I was already late for work.

At last, the heat blew across my toes. My foot hit the gas pedal, and I sped down the road.

When I reached my office, a note from my supervisor was taped to the door. "Come to my office as soon as you arrive."

I hurried down the hall and stood in her doorway.

Susan looked up. "Trudy, I know you're busy today, but I'm afraid you'll have to rearrange your schedule."

My heart sank. "Oh, no. What is it?"

"The Jordan children again." Her voice was filled with sadness.

"What happened now?" I couldn't hide the disgust in my voice. "Has nothing improved?"

"Apparently not. The neighbors called again. The children are in a bad state of neglect. The neighbors are growing weary of keeping them fed and clothed while the parents run around and leave them unattended. This morning Mr. Jordan called, asking us to come and get his kids. Again." Susan sighed. "His wife has left him for the third time, and he can't take care of them himself. Says we can take them all—he's fed up. I guess he feels like he can walk away from four children and never look back. Want me to go with you? No telling what you'll find when you get there."

"I can handle it."

By 9:00 a.m., I was headed down an almost impassable dirt road in the middle of nowhere. As my car bumped through the mud and the potholes, each house looked the same—houses almost falling down. They all looked like they should be condemned as uninhabitable.

I pulled up to the shack, and a chill ran down my spine. My hands shook. The last time I'd come here, the house had been empty, and I had to drive all over the community looking for the children. Mr. and Mrs. Jordan had dropped each child off at a different house, expecting the neighbors to take care of them and feed them for days while they drifted about. Today, the house was eerily quiet.

Where is everybody?

When no one responded to my knock, I opened the front door and stepped inside. The scent of urine took my breath away. My hand flew to my mouth in disbelief. Newspapers were scattered on the floor, as if someone had left an untrained dog alone in a house. Small forms appeared to be asleep on the floor atop the papers, with what looked like blood all around them.

The children. *Were they even alive?* I knew their names. David was the oldest at five, then Martha, Linda, and Wanda.

That's when I saw her. Wanda, the baby.

Tears flowed down my cheeks as I moved toward the youngest child. She lay still, clinging to a shredded, filthy blanket, in the bottom drawer of a tattered dresser. She wore only a soaking-wet cloth diaper. At first glance, I did not think she was alive. The paperwork indicated she was eight months old. She was so frail that I could see her ribs, and she shivered from the cold. A rope led from her feet and circled around one of the dresser's knobs.

Why would somebody tie up a baby?

As I untied the rope around her feet, she opened her eyes, whimpered, and reached for me. Taking off my sweater, I wrapped it around her and cradled her in my arms, burying her in my chest. Wanda's cries turned to screams.

I turned to see David, a small boy with sad, blue eyes. He tried to jump up when he saw me standing there, holding his baby sister, but he, too, was tied tightly to one of the chairs. His bloody fingers worked the rope, desperately trying to free his ankles. I knelt to help him, talking softly to calm him.

"David, honey, I'm here to help you. I'm a caseworker. I won't hurt you. Please trust me. It's going to be okay."

He stopped and began to sob.

"Is this your sister?" I pointed to the other small form on the floor as she began to stir. Her foot, sticking out from a dirty sheet, was also tethered with a rope.

That had to be Martha, the four-year-old. "Martha, sweetie. Don't be afraid."

I took a small pair of scissors from my purse and set her free. Martha was weak and dehydrated. They all needed food and water, but I realized there was no water in the house.

Linda. Where was Linda?

I held the baby close to my chest and reached for Martha's hand, pulling her close.

"David, do you know where Linda is?" The paperwork said Linda was only two years old.

David's glance moved behind me. His shaking finger pointed to the corner of the room behind another dirty sheet, this one hanging on a rod.

"Dare. She's in dare."

I turned to look, the blood still fresh on the floor. I pulled back the sheet, and the screeching sound caused Wanda to jerk and peer up at me. Linda's feet were also bound, her ankles bruised and bleeding. She looked so cold lying on the bare floor.

Still holding onto Martha's hand, I rushed to her. "Linda!"

She didn't move. I glanced at David and Martha and saw the fear in their eyes.

"Linda." I touched her dirty toes.

At the sound of the baby coughing, Linda opened her eyes. She too was extremely thin and cold.

"Linda, it's going to be okay, honey. I'm here to help."

The ropes were so tight that I asked David to hold Wanda. Kneeling, I used my scarf to clean Linda's ankles. Her wounds were deep. I took my time cutting the ropes that dug into her skin.

Linda flinched in pain but remained still and quiet. She must have been in shock.

Finally, she was free. I looked at each of them in turn. Their clothes were soiled with urine and blood from being left alone and tied for hours.

"We've got to get out of here."

I carried Linda to my car. Spreading my coat on the back seat, I gently placed her there. Still holding Wanda, David walked behind me and slid in next to Linda while Martha quietly followed. They curled up in the seat together, like abandoned puppies. No fight left. I could see it in their eyes, they seemed grateful to be found.

I looked over the hood of my car at that house.

This is the worst case of abuse and neglect I have ever witnessed.

Back at the office, I laid on my horn for someone to help. The other caseworkers came running.

"Get Marjorie and Susan. I'm going to need at least three of you to help me with these children."

Stephanie ran back into the office, hollering as she went. "Come quick, it's the Jordan children. They're in bad shape. Get some clean washcloths, towels, and clothes."

I passed over Wanda when Stephanie returned. "Give her a warm bath. She's coughing a lot. She must be very sick."

Stephanie gagged when I handed Wanda to her. "I'm so sorry, Trudy."

When she changed Wanda's diaper, she discovered a severe case of diaper rash. Deep open wounds—bed sores on an eight-month-old baby.

"Poor children. It wouldn't surprise me if they're all sick, living in those conditions. I know we are not supposed to judge the parents, but, ugh!" Marjorie muttered the words as she took David's hand and led him inside.

"Let's just focus on cleaning them up," I said, ushering everyone into the building. "Call the doctor. The oldest girl is definitely sick too. She's burning up. Her cough sounds deep, like pneumonia. She probably needs to be hospitalized. The baby will surely be in the hospital soon as well. When she's not crying, she's coughing."

When everything was handled, I excused myself to the bathroom.

I rushed into a stall and locked the door as I began to weep. I covered my face with my hands. When I looked up, I noticed my hands were red—covered with the children's blood.

Wiping my face clean with tissue, I tried to compose myself by taking deep breaths. I unlocked the bathroom stall door and walked to the mirror. My blue sweater was covered in black grime and streaks of blood, my pencil skirt wrinkled and torn.

Stephanie called from the hall. "Trudy, the doctor's here. He needs you now. Can you come into your office right away?"

"I'm all done." I ran out with hands dripping wet. "Where are the children?"

Stephanie put her arm around me. "Are you okay?"

"It's not about me." I shrugged her off and started down the hall. "It's about the children. Where's the doctor?"

In the back room, Dr. Wilson listened to Wanda's lungs with his stethoscope pressed against her chest.

"This one needs to be hospitalized immediately," he said. "Let me check the next child. Oh, God."

One by one he listened to their heart and lungs, his face a mask of concern.

"Call the ambulance," he told me. "There's no time to waste."

I turned to Stephanie and Marjorie. "Start the paperwork. I'm going in the ambulance with them. We must locate the parents and get them to sign the papers immediately, get our legal department working on that emergency hearing. This one needs to be set as quickly as possible."

Hours later, after the children were safe at the hospital, I returned to the office.

Marjorie came into my office and closed the door. "Trudy, I've been trying all morning to locate the parents, but since they have no phone, it's hard to figure out where they might be. I'm afraid we're going to have return to the house and wait for them."

I frowned. "Mr. Jordan is a house painter by trade, but I don't know where he's working. Can you go back out there with me to talk with him? The way I'm feeling right now, I don't want to go alone."

"Sure, but you may have to pull me off him if I lose my temper too." Marjorie shook her head, then gave me the once over.

I looked down at my clothes, covered in dirt and blood, and winced. "May I borrow a change of clothes and a coat?"

"Of course. I'll find you something in the clothes closet."

When we arrived at the house, I parked my car on the opposite side, so it would not be seen immediately. Marjorie and I sat in my car, turning on the engine occasionally to keep warm.

Around 4:00 p.m., Mr. Jordan drove up the dirt road in a beat-up old truck. He didn't seem to notice my car.

Marjorie and I got out of the car as he walked to the front door, watching as he stood in the doorway with his back to us. His children were not where he'd left them.

He turned around, expression blank. "Where'd you take 'em? I guess you got papers for me to sign."

The stench of alcohol on his breath made me nauseous.

"Mr. Jordan, your children are now in the custody of the Department of Public Welfare. Yes, we do have papers for you and Mrs. Jordan to sign. Today." Holding back my anger, I handed him the papers.

"Well, I'll sign whatever you got, but good luck finding her!" He laughed and shook his head. "Don't think she's coming back. Last she told me, she was moving to North Carolina with another man."

Our eyes met.

He cocked his head at me. "You cut 'em loose, huh? I had to work. Had no choice but to tie 'em up so they couldn't get out of the house. Nobody wants 'em anymore. I asked the neighbors—they don't want 'em either. What was I s'posed to do?"

My face stung with anger. "I told you the last time I was here, Mr. Jordan. You could have brought the children to DPW. You didn't have to tie them up like that. There's no excuse for this abuse. We're here to help you when you need us. You can tell the judge why you did this. Sign these papers so the Department of Public Welfare can care for your children until they may be placed in foster care, awaiting a court date."

"Here." He smirked as he threw the papers at me. His signature was scribbled and illegible, but sufficient.

Marjorie and I rushed to my car.

My hands shook as I fumbled to put the key in the ignition. "Let's get out of here." I jerked the car into drive and left a trail of dust as I sped away.

At the office, I called my most dependable foster caregivers. Could they take one more child? I hated to split up the siblings, but right now, I wanted them to have the best care so they could thrive—and they needed special attention.

I called the pastor of a local church first. The phone rang twice, and with each ring, I felt my heart leap in my chest. "Please answer the phone," I whispered.

"Hello?" Reverend Black's voice sounded like an old sea captain's—raspy and resonant. His voice felt like a warm embrace.

"Reverend Black, I know you have three foster children, but I have two girls, eight months and almost three years old. They're being removed from a ghastly situation. I can't go into much detail without crying, so I'll just say this. The baby probably has pneumonia and will need hospitalization until she is well again. The three-year-old will need to learn what a bathroom is and how to use it. Oh, Reverend Black …" I choked back a sob.

"Trudy, I'm here when you need me. Let me know when they're released."

"Reverend Black, this is definitely the worst case I've ever witnessed."

"Get some rest, Trudy, and call me back tomorrow, dear."

I took a deep breath as I hung up the phone.

God in heaven, help me. Okay, who else should I call?

Mrs. McTeer and Mrs. Gardner were next. After each call, I made notes of who needed what medical care and clothes, as well as any special needs the child had. The lists were long. The boy would go to one home and the oldest girl to the other when she was discharged. She, too, had pneumonia.

My last phone call for the night was to the hospital. It was 10:15 p.m.

"I'd like to check on the Jordan children."

"One moment, please."

Struggling to keep my eyes open, I waited.

"Hello, this is Nurse Sarah."

"Sarah, this is Trudy Melton from DPW. How are the Jordan children tonight?"

"I've checked on both girls, Ms. Trudy. The oldest girl, Martha, is still very sick. Her pneumonia is severe. She'll need to stay with us for some time. Linda's wounds on her ankles are bandaged and will need to be changed frequently. She has an IV for fluids because of dehydration. Wanda, the baby, is also very sick. High fever, terrible cough. We are desperately trying to control both of those symptoms. It's unclear at this time how long she'll have to stay in the hospital." Sarah's voice dropped. "Physically, David is doing the best, but emotionally, he's a wreck. He panics any time he's separated from his sisters. We're trying to console him. His fingers are bandaged, but he's responding well to treatment. The doctor will see them all in the morning."

My heart clutched. "Is Martha saying anything?"

Sarah took a deep breath. When she spoke again, I could hear the shattered tone in her voice.

"Ms. Trudy, who would do this to their own children?" She paused as if she were swallowing a marble lodged deep in her throat. "Martha keeps asking for her sisters. I tell her they're fine, that she will see them very soon, but she's so scared."

"Thank you, Sarah, for watching over them tonight. God bless you."

"I'm on the night shift. I won't leave their sides. You get some rest now yourself, Ms. Trudy."

I still didn't feel victory for these children. My goal now was to ensure Mr. Jordan and his wife never saw them again.

After a restless night, I came in early to work the next day, eager to get done quickly.

I went straight to my desk and picked up the phone.

"Marjorie, I hate to disturb you at home so early, but we need to get out to the Jordan house by 7:00 a.m., before Mr. Jordan leaves for his job. Bill, the process server, is heading over there now. I'll meet you there." I gritted my teeth. "Mr. Jordan is not going to get out of facing a judge. I'll make sure of that if it's the last thing I do."

"Sure." Marjorie sounded as angry as I was. "I wouldn't miss this for the world."

I yanked my keys off the desk, heading toward my car like a horse to the finish line. My blood pressure rose as I slid into the driver's seat.

"He'll see his day in court." I gritted my teeth.

I could drive this route with my eyes closed. Each time I had felt fear, sorrow, and anger. Today, it was going be vengeance.

I could only imagine what this road had felt like for those pitiful children.

When I arrived at the Jordan house, Bill was already there, parked right behind an old beat-up blue Ford truck. The bed was filled with ladders, and paint was splattered like confetti across the sides of the truck.

Bill had positioned his car so the truck was blocked. He got out with a look of anger on his face.

Mr. Jordan stood a few feet away from the truck, arms crossed.

I don't know what I'd do without Bill. A huge man in stature, he's built like a bouncer at a nightclub. He kept his long ponytail neatly combed. The muscles on his arms alone would scare anyone. He looked gruff, but I knew his heart. He had a deep love for children and could easily cause great bodily harm to a man if he didn't hold his anger in check, especially when he encountered abuse like this.

I parked my car behind Bill's.

"Mr. Jordan," Bill's deep voice called out.

"Yeah, who wants to know?"

"I'm here to serve you, sir."

"Serve me what?"

"This is an order to appear in court, sir, to answer the complaint filed against you."

"What complaint?"

"Mr. Jordan, that's for you to read and find out, as if you don't know." Bill strode to Mr. Jordan and put the papers in his hand.

Then Bill walked over to me.

"He's all yours now, Trudy, but I'm going to stick around if that's all right with you," he whispered. "I don't trust this guy any further than I can spit."

I gave Bill a quick pat on the back. "Thanks, hon," I whispered.

Bill and I had worked together on many cases. He was always there when I needed him, at a moment's notice. Just recently, I'd had to call him in the middle of a cold December night to rescue a child who'd been left on a church doorstep. That night I had consoled Bill more than he had comforted me.

But this time, I sensed his rage. He'd have been looking for an opportunity to deck Mr. Jordan if I hadn't been standing there. One blow from Bill's fist and Mr. Jordan's head would be spinning with dizziness.

I looked at Mr. Jordan. For such an angry man, he wasn't intimidating. Rather skinny and sheepish looking and much shorter than I expected. He had a temper, though, that could burst out at any moment, especially fueled with alcohol—I'd seen it.

He looked through the papers, not really reading them, more like questioning what they meant. He held them up toward the sun, as if they were an ancient text or a secret map.

I was baffled. "Mr. Jordan, sir, can you read the papers?"

I thought back to the night before as I was reading the case history on this family. The file noted Mr. Jordan had only a third-grade education. A folder marked "Confidential" contained a report from the Greenville Mental Health Center, which stated he'd been arrested once for "peeping into a neighbor's home, naked himself." He'd been ordered to see a mental health specialist but never followed through with the order.

"Yes, I can read." Still, he continued to flip the pages.

Knowing what I knew, I had to be sure he understood.

"The papers say you must appear before the judge on July 1, 1957, to explain why … why you abused and neglected your children."

The last words bellowed out of me before I could stop them. I could almost see the wind carry them, as if they were small pieces of glass trying to pierce his heart.

Mr. Jordan didn't look at me. He simply folded the papers and put them in his back pocket.

"All right then. Can I go to work now?"

I felt Bill's hand on me, like he was trying to hold me back. "You've done all you can do now, Trudy. Let him go," Bill whispered.

I took a deep breath and turned away.

The next few months were a blur. I threw myself into work, determined to find the mother who'd abandoned these babies. She may have thought she'd gotten away, but I intended to show her otherwise. Wherever she was, I'd find her, and she would stand before a judge.

And neither she, nor the father, would ever get those kids back.

It's hard to believe it took us two months to locate her. Mr. Jordan finally admitted he knew her address, and we immediately served her with court papers to relinquish her parental rights so her children could be released for adoption. But, to my surprise, she refused to consent to allow her children to be adopted or put in an orphanage, even though she knew she could not support them.

I obtained a court order that the Jordans pay board for all children while they were in foster care. Of course, they never paid a cent.

Martha, the oldest girl, was eventually released from the hospital and put in foster care. While it was a separate home from the other two girls, I placed her in the same home with her brother. At least two of them were together, for a while.

Initially, Mr. Jordan insisted he was ready to sign papers for all his children to be adopted. He realized his marriage was over, and he couldn't afford to support them. Then he changed his mind, as if he should have any leverage in the matter at all. He refused to sign papers for the two oldest children. He said he would agree to putting them in an orphanage nearby and, when they got older, the oldest girl could come back home and "keep house" for him.

I almost threw up in front of him.

Mrs. Jordan seemed terrified at that scenario, as if she could imagine the awful things that would happen to her daughter if he were allowed to keep her. She adamantly refused to sign any papers to give her children back to him, claiming he was an "abusive alcoholic" and "a danger to the children."

A few months later, both parents again stood before a judge. The mother signed the papers relinquishing her parental rights and agreeing to release all four children for adoption.

But when the father came into the courtroom, while he was willing to relinquish parental rights to the two youngest children, freeing them to be adopted, he claimed to be making realistic plans to keep the two older children.

Everything had stalled.

The children all remained in foster care the entire next year. The father paid child support a few times, but then stopped, saying he "couldn't afford it anymore." The court halved the fee to twenty-five dollars a month. He never paid it. He was incarcerated for nonpayment of child support, yet he insisted he didn't want to release the two older children, David and Martha, for adoption. Linda and Wanda, the two youngest, remained in separate foster homes.

Fortunately for the two youngest girls, the story has a happy ending. We were able to find a loving home for both of them, and they were adopted together on August 15, 1958.

Life did not go as well for the two oldest. While DPW records reflected both of them should have been released for adoption, the father refused to relinquish his parental rights to them, promising the court that he was making plans for them to be returned to him.

In 1963, the foster mother of the two older children became ill. Against the recommendation of DPW, the court returned them to the custody of their father—what would turn out to be, for Martha, a grave mistake. From August 1963 to March 1964, Martha remained with her father. We later discovered her father physically abused her the whole time. Martha begged DPW to allow her to return to the foster home, and in March 1964, her plea was heard.

David, however, refused to return to the foster home, claiming they had beaten him. The DPW allowed him to remain with his father.

The DPW continued to monitor Martha in foster care until she was eighteen. At that time, she married, and the foster care case was closed.

As for me, I'm still haunted by nightmares of what happened to these four precious children. Their situation remains the worst case of physical abuse and neglect I ever encountered.

Wanda at courthouse April 1958

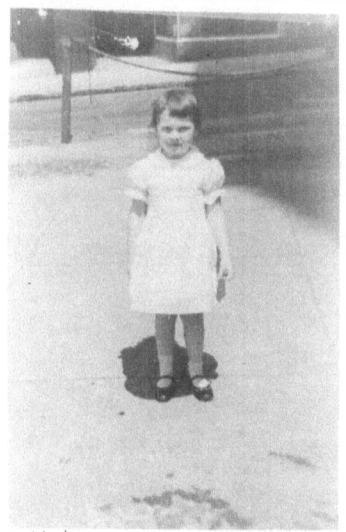

Linda at courthouse April 1958

The Long Road

I'm a nervous wreck, and I want everything to be perfect.

August 15, 1958
Lydia, South Carolina
Adoptive Parents

"Carwell, can you hand me my dress? The one with the gold buttons?" Frances called out from the bathroom, her voice trembling with nerves and excitement.

"Sure, hon."

With a towel around her hair, Frances peeked out, smiling at her husband as he handed her the dress he'd bought her to wear that day. He gazed at his wife, still lovely. With her olive complexion, navy blue looked good on her.

The graze of her fingertips on his took Carwell back to the day they'd met, all those years ago.

Police Chief V. C. Elmore Sr. had visited Carwell's family home out in the country to buy chickens. While he'd had no idea Chief Elmore had such a beautiful daughter, Carwell's respectful attitude and good manners had apparently made a big impression that day on the chief.

When the chief returned home with the chickens, he mentioned the young man he'd met out in the country.

"I believe his name is Carwell." The chief had turned to his daughter-in-law, Mildred. "Do you know him?"

"Yes, I met him too, not so long ago when I went out to buy some eggs. He's never been married!" Mildred grinned, eying her sister-in-law. "I know you'd like him, Frances. How about going on a double date with us next weekend? I'll go out there and talk with him for you."

Frances had shaken her head reluctantly but smiled—and agreed.

Carwell later learned that Frances had been awestruck by him, and as for him, he was completely overwhelmed by her beauty. Very shy, he felt somewhat unequal to her. Frances was a high school graduate, but Carwell had only finished the third grade. His father had been ill most of his life and, as the eldest of three, Carwell had to quit school early to work the farm.

Luckily for him, Frances looked beyond the surface of a man to his heart, and his good, kind heart impressed her the most.

They dated for several years before tying the knot July 24, 1953.

But Frances had a serious thyroid disease, and doctors had removed most of her thyroid gland. Even though they prayed for children, Frances had never been able to conceive. After five years, the conversation turned to adoption.

One day, Frances looked at Carwell and said, with sadness in her voice, "Let's go ahead and fill out the papers for adoption."

Carwell instantly agreed. "I think that would be a good thing to do. So many babies need a home, and maybe that's what we're supposed to do."

The day of the appointment with the social worker finally came, and the couple waited anxiously to meet with her. After reviewing their paperwork for a long time, the social worker, Betty, called them back into her office.

Her expression indicated bad news. "Unfortunately, you've both reached the ages where you're no longer eligible to adopt an infant. However, you may still adopt a child, one who's a little older, just not a baby."

Carwell and Frances held hands, unsure how to react.

"Here," the social worker continued, pointing toward a large album on her shelf. "Let me show you this book of available children who desperately need the stability of a loving home."

Carwell had looked at Frances, trying to gauge her feelings. "We hadn't thought about an older child, but I suppose we could look at some pictures."

Frances was overwhelmed.

"This is too much for me to think about right now," Frances said, her lips quivering. "May we go back home to think and pray about it for a few days?"

"Certainly. I don't expect you to decide today." The social worker gave them a kind smile. "Take your time."

The ride home was quiet as they contemplated their future.

"What do you think, Carwell?" Frances finally broke the silence.

"Well, she's right," Carwell said as he drove. "We are a little older than most parents first seeking adoption. I have no problem with adopting an older child, but not one who might be a lot of trouble later in life."

"Yes. That would be hard."

A few days passed, and they returned to their normal routines. One Sunday after church, Frances mentioned to her mother that they were considering adoption.

"That would be wonderful!" Frances's mother, Elise, smiled at her daughter. "I've been reading about how many abused and neglected children are left in orphanages. I'm sure God would honor you and Carwell in this decision and send you an angel of a child to love."

Frances and Carwell discussed the possibility for many hours.

The next day, Frances called the social worker.

"Okay," she told her, squeezing Carwell's hand. "We'd like to look into adopting a young child. May we come back and look at the pictures again?"

"Of course. Would two o'clock this afternoon work?"

"See you then." Frances hung up the phone and grabbed Carwell around the neck, crying tears of joy.

"We're really going to do this?"

"Yes, let's do it."

At their appointment, the social worker struggled with the large album in her arms.

"This photo album is full of pictures. As you can see, many boys and girls await adoption. Look over these, and if you have any questions, let me know. I'll be right outside."

She exited the room.

"Well, here we go." Frances smiled as they opened the photo album.

They turned the pages for a long time and kept going back to one little girl with sad eyes. They both agreed: She was the one.

"We've made a decision," Frances called out to the caseworker, who came back into the room. "But we'd like to ask a few questions."

"What's this little girl's story? Carwell asked, pointing to her picture. "She seems so small and sad."

The caseworker took a deep breath. "Her name's Wanda. She's only three years old, and she's been in foster care since she was eight months old. She is very shy around strangers and quite withdrawn." She pointed to the picture next to Wanda's. "That's Linda, her sister. She's five. She, too, has been in foster care most of her life."

Frances and Carwell stared at the pictures, imagining what the two girls had experienced.

"I'm afraid we can't separate them," the caseworker said. "The older one is very protective of her little sister, and since they've been together in the children's home, they've been inseparable. Linda won't eat all her food sometimes because she wants to save some for her sister. We think it's best if they stay together."

She gave them a smile. "Would you be interested in taking them both?"

Carwell and Frances looked at each other, eyes wide.

"Yes!" Carwell said.

"We wouldn't think of separating them," Frances added, nodding.

"Great! But you need to know the whole story. Let me pull the file and go over all the details. But one important thing." The caseworker's voice was grave. "Wanda may be going blind. She rolls her eyes back in her head when anyone approaches her. A pediatrician or optometrist will have to check to see if she can focus her eyes."

Carwell shook his head. "I'd rather keep her myself and raise her blind than send her back and wonder all my life what happened to her."

The smile on Frances's face showed great pride in her husband.

They sat for hours completing all the paperwork and then waited months until the adoption was finalized.

Finally, the day to adopt the girls arrived. Carwell sat in the living room, trying to calm his pounding heart. A family, at last.

As Frances stepped from the bathroom, the scent of lavender and roses rushed to meet him. Carwell knew how much today meant to Frances—to them both. Neither had slept much the night before. They must have made up the girls' brand-new twin beds five times last night.

He sensed her heartfelt emotion, and it was infectious. Five long years they'd waited. The paperwork, the disappointments, and the lengthy interviews had all led to this day.

The night before, Carwell had laid a map out on their bed, planning the best route to take and tracing it with a red ballpoint pen. Drawing a line from Lydia to Greenville, he determined it was about a two-hour drive. He placed stars beside the rest stops on the way back in case the girls needed bathroom breaks or were hungry. He wanted to be fully prepared.

"Well, how do I look?" Frances entered the living room.

"Beautiful." He fiddled with his tie again. "Is it straight?"

Although Frances told him all the time he resembled Humphrey Bogart, he was a plant worker and a farmer by trade, and dressing in a suit was awkward for him. But today everything had to be perfect.

Frances grinned at him. "So handsome. I think I'll keep you."

On this fifteenth day of August 1958, the thermometer read 104 degrees. Carwell had spent hours the previous day polishing and cleaning his 1958 Ford Fairlane 500. He paid cash for his new cars, saving every extra penny from the sale of a hog or the profits from a good tobacco crop to buy them. This year's bumper tobacco crop enabled him to buy his family—his family, and soon these precious little girls—that big black-and-white beauty of an automobile.

"Here are the stuffed animals and baby dolls," he said, his arms full. "Let's put them on the back dashboard so the girls can choose which ones they want to play with. That will keep them occupied on the long ride home."

"Oh, no! Carwell!" Frances shrieked.

Carwell jumped, dropping his wallet in the mud puddle. "What is it, Frances? You scared me to death."

"I've pulled a run in my stockings. I've got to go inside and change." Frances darted for the house, slamming the screen door behind her.

Shaking his head and hiding his smile, Carwell picked up his soggy wallet and wrapped it in a handkerchief to dry.

Finally, she returned, out of breath from running. "Okay, I'm ready!" She slid into the car seat. "Let's go!"

"Take a deep breath and calm down, Frances. We have plenty of time. We are way ahead of schedule." Carwell patted her on her back.

"I'm sorry." Frances leaned her head back on the car seat. "I'm a nervous wreck, and I want everything to be perfect."

"It will be, hon." Carwell softly rubbed her shoulder. "It will be."

Turning the key in the ignition, they slowly backed out of the driveway.

Something in Their Eyes

Who would be chosen today?

August 15, 1958
Greenville, South Carolina
Linda

"Smile," a lady said as she clicked the button on a camera.

I jumped, frightened at each click, my mouth curved in a determined frown. There was nothing to smile about.

At five years old, I had already learned to read people's faces, and I knew something was happening today. I stood in the parking lot of a huge, stone building as the lady took my picture. She grabbed me by the hand and led me back inside the orphanage. My eyes moved back and forth as I watched and listened. Everyone moved around like bees in a hive—gathering, collecting, and cleaning to impress some potential family.

Who would be chosen today?

I perched on the edge of my bed and played with the corners of my dress, poking my fingers through the holes around the hem. I tried to sit still, but my heart pounded. The broken bedsprings squeaked with each move I made. Footsteps grew louder in the hall. Some of the other girls looked anxious too, but none of us spoke. We sat silent, looking at one another. One of the younger nurses rushed in.

"Come on now. We've got to get you cleaned up." She snatched my hand and hurried me out the door and down to the orphanage bathroom.

"Linda, get in the tub." Her eyes pleaded with me.

"The water's too cold!" I complained as I stuck my foot in the water.

The nurse ignored me. I squeezed my eyes shut against the sting of the dripping soap. She dumped the cold water over my head with a white pail. The water turned from clear to musky yellow as the dirt ran off me. I wanted to sit and play a bit, even in my filth, but there was no time for that.

The nurse whisked me out of the tub and rubbed me down with a scratchy old towel.

"Be still. This will only take a second." She opened a drawer, took out a huge pair of rusty scissors, and then began to cut my long, dark hair.

Tears rolled down my cheeks as I watched each clump of hair drop to the floor.

Another nurse walked toward me. She held two white bows, one in each hand. She put one in my hair and set the other on the table next to me. They whispered something about another girl.

I wanted to know who that bow was for, but I was too afraid to ask.

Was it for my sister? Was Wanda going to wear that bow?

A pretty pale-blue dress hung on a nail on the back of the bathroom door.

"Put your feet in here," the nurse instructed as she slid a pair of panties up my legs.

Forcing a slip over my head, she said, "Hold your arms up and quit your squirming. We gotta hurry."

She pulled the thin blue dress over my head and tied the bow in the back. I hid my smile.

I felt so fancy. I wanted to spin in circles, but instead I sat and waited quietly. Beside the chair were two shiny new white shoes. I had never seen shoes like that.

They can't be for me.

"Well, ain't you gonna put on them shoes?" The nurse crossed her arms and glared at me. Placing each one in front of a foot, I slid my toes in. They hurt, but they were the prettiest shoes I'd ever seen. I knew better than to complain.

Minutes passed as I waited. All the other girls had gone to breakfast. The sound of the door startled me, and I turned to see my baby sister. Now I could smile.

Wanda, just three years old, was holding the hand of an old nurse and standing in the doorway. She was all cleaned up and wearing that other bow. The nurse's huge, wrinkled hands pushed Wanda through the door.

"Go on now, sit with your sister and be quiet." I knew she noticed my mean look at her for treating my sister like that. I narrowed my eyes … how dare she speak to Wanda that way. With her head down and eyes rolled back, my little sister didn't look up to see me at first.

"Wanda." I reached out for her hand. "It's me. It's Finn." I used the old nickname, the one I knew she loved.

Wanda looked up and smiled.

"You're gonna be okay, Sissy. I'm here now."

She ran to grab my hand.

Another nurse came in and took us to an empty waiting room. The bare white walls gave us nothing to look at except, on the wall above the table, a picture of a guardian angel watching over two children crossing a bridge. The angel's gown glowed, illuminating the path to the other side. Closing my eyes, I wished Wanda and I could become the children in the picture.

The nurse sat us at the table under the angel picture. She handed me a piece of paper and a pencil.

"Here. Now mind your manners and keep quiet." Her harsh words lingered after she slammed the door behind her.

Wanda was so scared. As I watched, she withdrew into her own world. I always wondered where she went and what her world was like. She could always escape into a safe, happy place in her mind when she was sad or scared.

I drew rainbows and flowers with my pencil, attempting to create a world on paper where we could be happy together.

Wanda had not spoken since we were placed here months ago. The nurses didn't understand her silence and kept taunting her, trying to make her speak.

"She lost her words!" I had yelled at them. I knew how she felt. Sometimes I forgot things too. Life was easier that way.

The door opened. I looked up at the most beautiful lady I'd ever seen. She glowed like an angel, like the one in the picture. Her dark hair was wavy, and her eyes were kind. Standing next to her was a man dressed in a dark suit. He smiled and knelt to speak to us, eye to eye.

Next to them, the caseworker said, "Girls, I have someone I want you to meet."

Wanda shrunk back, and I pulled her close.

"Linda, Wanda, this is Mr. and Mrs. Haney. I'll leave you alone for a few minutes."

At first, Wanda clung tightly to me, but she started to retreat into her world again as she loosened her grip. Her body was still in my arms, but her eyes rolled back in her head. On the outside, as my eyes met theirs, I smiled at the couple, but on the inside, I wondered why they were there.

I realized they were different somehow than the others I'd met. I felt kindness in their expressions. I was not used to kindness. My fears subsided. I wanted so badly to trust them. I knew that I had to stay strong, smile, and welcome this man and woman into our lives. I had to—for Wanda. For both of us.

Mr. Haney spoke softly. "Girls, would you like to go for a ride out into the country? We have a farm with cows, dogs, and a couple of cats. I built a new swing set and a sandbox you can play in too."

Mrs. Haney gazed at me, a smile on her lips. "Linda, would you like to come with us?"

I blinked, suddenly worried. "I can't go anywhere without my sister."

"Don't worry, dear." Mrs. Haney's voice sounded like ice cream. "You'll never be separated again."

I took Wanda's face in my hand and lifted her chin. "Did you hear that?"

I watched as she moved out of her world and back into mine.

Wanda looked at me and smiled. Yes.

"Yes, ma'am," I said, and then smiled. "We'll go."

With our hands interwoven like braided twine, Wanda and I walked side by side. This wasn't the first time we had been all dressed up, but something about this day felt different. Something in the Haneys' eyes felt like home. When the orphanage door opened, a large black and white car was waiting for us.

Mr. Haney walked to the car and opened the back door. "Go ahead, girls. Those are for you."

The back seat was filled with toys. Without hesitation, I jumped in. "Wanda, look! New baby dolls."

I looked up at Mr. and Mrs. Haney. "Thank you!"

"You're very welcome," they said in unison, looking at each other and laughing.

"Linda, why don't you come up here in the front seat with me, and Wanda, you can sit in the back seat with Mrs. Haney."

I tried to reassure Wanda. "You sit with Mrs. Haney. The back seat has lots of room, and I'm right up here."

The car door shut. Wanda stood and called out to me.

"Finn, Finn!"

I reached back and held her hand. "It's okay, Sissy."

After a few minutes, the hum of the motor calmed Wanda. Settling her head on Mrs. Haney's lap, she fell asleep. While Mr. Haney drove, I studied him, listening to the breaths he took. I watched the trees, each of them waving goodbye.

"Where are the trees going?" I asked.

"The trees are not moving, sweetheart. We are." Mr. Haney smiled as he brushed my hair with his hand.

"Oh, I see that now."

I rested my head on the door until I, too, surrendered to sleep.

The sound of gravel and brakes awakened us. Mr. Haney opened the car door, and Wanda ran into my arms. We stood still and looked around.

Where are we?

Mrs. Haney held out her hand. "Come, girls, let us show you around."

I noticed the light in her eyes. They were brown and sparkled with shades of copper in the afternoon sun.

I took Wanda by the hand once more. We were scared, but we found safety in the warmth of each other's hands. The farm was vast, and I felt so small in this grand design of hills and pastures. In the distance, I saw cows. They looked like black and brown specks on the hills.

Mr. Haney pointed out to them and turned to me. "Child, see? Those are the cows I told you about."

I smiled as I looked up at his gentle face.

"Let's go to the swing set I built."

"I can swing some, but my sister is little. She could fall."

"That's okay, hon," Mrs. Haney said. "She can play in the sandbox."

I slid into the swing, my feet lifting off the ground.

"May I push you?" Mr. Haney asked.

"Yes, sir." I reached my toes to the clouds. "My sister might like the seesaw."

"Let's give it a try, Wanda," he said.

I jumped off the swing and helped Wanda onto the seesaw. Playing peek-a-boo with her as we swung back and forth, we giggled.

Holding in her tears, Mrs. Haney put her hand over her mouth as she watched us play.

Later, we walked back toward the house.

"We have someone else for you to meet," Mrs. Haney said.

As we walked into the house, questions went through my mind again.

What does all this mean?

Who are these people?

Are we going to stay here?

Can I call them Mama and Daddy?

A beautiful older lady, fair and fragile, sat in an odd chair with two big wheels. Her dark hair was pulled back with bobby pins, her eyes full of kindness.

Stretching her arms wide, like the branches of big oak tree, she called out to us. "Well, hello girls, I'm so glad to meet you. I'm your grandmother. What's that you have there?"

"My new doll." I smiled at her. "Wanda got one too. And there were lots of other toys in the car."

"I see your beautiful new doll. I'm so glad you've come to stay with us. You'll be happy here."

"Come outside, girls. There's more for you to see." Mrs. Haney beckoned.

I took Wanda's hand, and we ran out the door to her.

But at the sight of a big dog, I stopped. "Stay back, Wanda!"

"Oh, Linda, he's a sweet dog. You don't have to be afraid." Mr. Haney patted the dog on his head.

I heard what he said, but fear washed over me. "I've never seen a good dog, Mr. Haney. Most of the time they growl at me and show their teeth."

"Not Bubba. Watch this—Bubba, sit."

To my surprise, Bubba sat obediently and presented his paw.

"Shake hands with him," Mr. Haney said. "That's his way of saying hi."

"Wow." I knelt and put out my hand, and Bubba put his head in my lap.

Wanda sat next to me and placed her hand on Bubba, a smile stretching across her face.

"He's a special breed of dog, an Australian Shepherd." Mr. Haney ruffled Bubba's hair. "The first time I saw him, I wanted him. His owner died recently, and one of his relatives told me Bubba needed a home, so I brought him here for you. He's a lot like you. Now he has a new home too."

I put my nose to Bubba's, brushed his pointed ears, and stared into his eyes.

"We're new here too, Bubba." He put his head on my knee, and I leaned in to whisper in his ear. "I love you."

"You girls hungry?" Mr. Haney asked.

"Yes, sir." My eyes grew big, and Wanda nodded.

"Let's go inside. I can smell fried chicken from here."

When we walked into the kitchen, the counter was filled with bowls of every color with all our favorites—macaroni and cheese, butter beans, rice and gravy, corn on the cob, and a basket full of homemade biscuits. Our eyes were like saucers as we looked around at the feast, grinning at each other.

The first evening in our new home, after playing outside for a long time, our new mom got us ready for bed. With a sparkle in her eye, she asked, "How about a hot bubble bath for you pretty girls?"

The idea of a hot bath puzzled me, but I didn't refuse and started to remove my clothes and shoes. Wanda copied me without a sound.

Mrs. Haney gasped. "Oh, dear, your shoes don't fit, do they?"

My feet had been numb since the morning, but I hadn't even noticed the blood and blisters on my toes until I looked down.

"No, ma'am. They hurt."

"Well, we best throw these away."

I smiled as she tossed them in the trash.

"Your bath is ready, girls. Go ahead and jump in."

As we did, she knelt and wiped up the bloody toe prints left on the floor.

As my body sank into the warm water, the past slid away. The days at the orphanage, with all the mean nurses and other children screaming, were over. There must have been days before the orphanage, but I didn't want to remember them.

The water got darker and darker from the dirt on my body. I imagined all my past being the dirt as I watched it disappear. Wanda and I played, splashed, and made bubble beards while Mrs. Haney scrubbed our matted hair.

I laughed at the sight of my wrinkled skin. "It looks like the nurses' skin!"

"That means it's time to dry off." Mrs. Haney grinned as she picked up a soft towel for each of us.

The smell of flowers filled my nose. This must be what Wanda's world smelled like—a world of fresh flowers and soft, warm towels.

Wrapped in our towels, we ran down the hall to our new bedroom, squealing all the way.

On each bed lay a new nightgown. Mine was long with tiny red roses scattered about. Wanda's was the same, with pink roses, and just her size. The beds had matching quilted blue covers. Our legs were covered with mosquito bites, and they itched so much. There were scabs from our scratching them. Before getting into bed, Mrs. Haney dabbed medicine on our cuts and pink lotion on our bites.

"This will make your legs feel much better. Now climb into bed, so I can tuck you in."

The sheets felt like a piece of silk I had found once on the orphanage floor, and the bed was so soft I sank into it as if it were a cloud.

I laid my head on my pillow and smelled the freshness of the sheets, like the air after it rained.

"May I sit with you girls for a while?" Wanda and I both nodded, and for the first time I could remember, there was no marching band in my head, no screaming children, just quiet. That night we quickly fell fast asleep.

#

The transition to our new home was difficult, especially for Wanda.

One evening in late August, the hot sun had finally set. The attic fan blew a cool evening breeze throughout the house.

Mrs. Haney tried everything she could think of to calm Wanda, but nothing worked.

Finally, Mr. Haney said, "Let me hold her."

He took her in his arms and walked out onto the screened porch, sat in the glider and swung back and forth.

Wiping the sweat from her forehead, Mrs. Haney smiled at me and took my hand.

"Come, dear, let Mr. Haney comfort your sister." She winked. "He's got the magic touch."

I sat on her lap in her favorite chair as she read a story.

Outside, Wanda could hardly lift her head. She spoke only one word: "Home."

Mr. Haney fought back tears and kept trying to reassure her. He repeated over and over, "You are home, honey. You belong here with me, Mama, your grandma, and your sister. We will never leave you."

After several hours of crying, she fell asleep in his arms.

I peeked out, and Mr. Haney patted the empty space next to him on the glider.

I tiptoed and took my place beside him. He kissed my head, and I laid my head on his knee.

Beside him on the glider, I pushed my fingers through the holes in the seat. With the smooth rhythm of the glider, my eyes grew heavy as I, too, drifted into a deep sleep. Later, they carried us to our beds.

This was the nightly ritual for our new daddy and mama. It was there on that glider we learned to feel safe. It was several weeks before Wanda and I learned to fall asleep in our beds.

Wanda and Daddy soon became inseparable.

After about a week of the bedtime ritual, one morning, Mrs. Haney called her husband.

"Carwell, come look."

"What is it?"

She pointed as they stood in our bedroom doorway. "We put them in their own beds each night, but every morning, this is what I find." She smiled as she wiped a tear from her cheek. "They are both in one bed with their hands tightly woven together as if they are afraid someone will take one of them during the night."

They embraced as they silently walked away.

One morning, as soon as Wanda and I awoke, we ran to the breakfast table.

"Good morning, Mama and Daddy," I grinned.

Their eyes grew big as they looked at each other and smiled.

That day, Mama told us it was time to go shopping.

"Shopping? What is that?" I asked.

"We will go to town, and you can pick out new clothes."

"Oh boy, oh boy!" We both jumped around the room.

As soon as we were dressed, we gave Bubba a big hug and kiss and ran to the car.

"Hello, girls," Mr. Rambo said as we entered the shoe store bearing his name. "Have a seat right here and let me see what size shoes you need."

We had never been in a shoe store, nor had our feet been measured. Wanda cried, fearful of Mr. Rambo touching her feet and sliding them into the huge measuring tool.

"It's okay, Wanda. Look, I'm going to get new shoes too," I promised her.

Soon she sat down again and allowed Mr. Rambo to measure her feet.

"Oh my," he said, looking up at our new mother. "No wonder they can't walk without falling. The shoes they're wearing are two sizes too small."

Somewhat embarrassed, Mama shook her head in disbelief. We left the store sporting beautiful black patent-leather shoes—shoes that fit.

Next, we went to Belk department store to buy new play clothes. We had a wonderful day shopping with our new mama.

Mama also loved to make our play clothes and dresses by hand on her sewing machine. I was so excited when she made dresses for my Barbie dolls that matched my clothes. In my eyes, Mama was a genius.

The ladies in the neighborhood and at the church were so excited about the adoption that they hosted a shower for Mama and Daddy and provided several new Peaches 'n Cream dresses for us to wear to church. I loved the full, crunchy slips, called crinolines, under the dresses.

Wanda and I had never been to church, at least, not that we could remember. Being the Christian woman she was, Mama made sure we were dressed in our new dresses and in church every Sunday.

One Sunday, Mama asked my new teacher, "How is Linda doing in Sunday school?"

"Oh, she's a sweet child. But she doesn't know yet how to sit still. Give her a little more time and she'll be fine."

Wanda was still too afraid to go to her own class, so she sat on Mama's lap in her class for a long time before she finally felt safe enough to go to class with me.

Early mornings, when Daddy was leaving for work, were hard for Wanda for a long time. "Wait, Daddy, wait!" Wanda cried out as she ran down the dirt road, little arms waving in the air and tears streaming down her face.

After he had worked third shift all night, he came home and climbed on his tractor to plow the fields before the sun was too hot. If he didn't slip out quietly, Wanda came running after him. He picked her up and put her on his knee as he plowed the fields, his arm tightly around her. She sat on his lap for hours as he worked. Sometimes I came too. Holding tightly onto Daddy's shoulders, giggling as the dust blew around us, we both loved to ride on the back of the old tractor.

#

Late one hot afternoon, someone knocked on the front door.

"Good afternoon, Mrs. Haney," said the kind voice on the other side.

It was Trudy Melton, the caseworker. She had stopped by for an unannounced visit to be sure we were being well taken care of in our new home.

Mama stood quickly. "Well, hello, Trudy! It's so nice to see you. I wasn't expecting you, so please excuse the mess."

Inevitably, it seemed, our caseworker always stopped by when Wanda and I had been out in the yard playing in the sand box and covered with dirt.

Trudy watched out the kitchen window as we played happily together.

"This is what I want to see," Trudy said, much to the relief of our new mother. "Two little girls getting dirty in the yard, but happy."

#

The hot summer soon ended, and the beautiful fall weather turned to winter. We celebrated our first Christmas in our new home.

Of course, there had been other Christmases, but not like this one. In the orphanage or in foster homes, our gifts had been used toys or raggedy dolls. Although grateful for anything, I knew our gifts were donations from local churches or from people who felt sorry for us.

This year, our gifts were from a mother and father who had hand-selected them for us, their new daughters.

"Linda, Wanda, wake up!" Daddy called on Christmas morning. "Come open your gifts."

Still in our pajamas, we ran screaming into the living room. Our eyes filled with tears as we saw our first brand-new Christmas toys: a child-size ironing board and iron, beautiful dolls, even my first tea set. We both got shiny new bikes too.

Never had we seen so many presents, purchased by a mother and father who truly loved us.

Wanda and I sat still on Mama's lap as she read from the Bible in Luke about the first Christmas. All we had ever been told about Christmas was that we had better be good or Santa would not bring us anything, but no one had ever told us that Jesus's birth was what Christmas was really about.

"Smile," Daddy said as he took picture after picture of us enjoying our first Christmas with our new mama, daddy, and grandmother.

This time, I smiled back at the camera, for I was no longer afraid. I jumped, but not in fright. I jumped for joy into my new daddy's loving arms.

#

Shortly after coming to our new home, we were taken to the pediatrician for a physical.

"Dr. Price, the Department of Public Welfare told me and Carwell that Wanda may be going blind. Can you take a look into her eyes and give me your opinion?"

After reviewing the shot records from DPW, indicating we had recently been given all our shots, the pediatrician examined Wanda's eyes.

"No, Mrs. Haney," he shook his head as he turned to her. "There's nothing wrong with this little girl's eyes—nothing that a little bit of love won't cure."

First day of adoption Aug. 1958

JUL • 59 •

NOV • 58

Grandma Elise

God wanted me to find you.

August 1958
Lydia, South Carolina
Linda

L ate one evening, lightning pierced the sky like a knife on fire. Thunder crawled through the darkness like a ghost.

"Grandma!" Wanda and I both shrieked as we ran down the hall to her bedroom.

"Come here, girls." She held out her arms to us and we jumped into her lap. Rocking us back and forth, she softly sang and whispered in our ears.

"Don't be afraid, girls. God is just watering all the beautiful trees and flowers. Let's sing praises to Him and thank Him. Remember what His Word says. "Whenever I'm afraid, I will put my trust in You," she would quote.

Her velvet alto voice echoed throughout the house as she sang "Jesus Loves Me." The fear of the unknown, which caused our insecurities to run deep, melted away. No one calmed our fears like Grandma.

The fear of abandonment caused deep anxiety to creep into our hearts. We didn't understand it at the time. I could always feel it move through my mind as I prepared for the worst. How I would keep my sister safe and with me was always my greatest fear. But, in Grandma's arms, or by her side, I knew we were both safe.

Elise Mathis Elmore, my wonderful, godly grandmother, was the most beautiful, kind lady I have ever known. I truly believe she was the reason God plucked me out of a horrible life and gave her to me. We were supposed to be together. Our bond was inseparable from the moment we met. With deep brown eyes and her olive complexion, Grandma lit up a room with her broad, sweet smile.

I recall with fondness the day I heard music coming from the living room. Wanda and I ran to see what that beautiful sound was. It was our grandmother! She was playing the piano so gracefully that we quietly climbed up on the couch to listen.

"Girls, come join me as I play you a song."

Her swollen knuckles and twisted fingers danced gracefully across the keys, the notes moved through me like waves moving through water.

Wanda and I would often snuggle up on the couch, her head on my shoulder. The calming sounds of the piano helped us relax.

Day stretched into evening. The warm glow of the sun setting casted its light and shadows across the living room floor. In the distance we could see the cows grazing their evening dinner, and the aroma of biscuits baking tickled our senses.

I have no doubt in my mind that God selected this family for me. It would have been easy for me to feel unlovable because I already believed someone didn't love me enough to keep me. My grandmother's face glowed with excitement every time she saw me come into a room. She taught me that God had a better plan for my life than anything I had already experienced or could imagine.

Before bedtime, she'd always cradle us in her arms like cherished children in a gentle hug and say, "God wanted *me* to find *you*."

The next morning, I heard her calling. "Linda, hon, I hate to ask you to help me, but I need to use the bedpan."

"No problem, Grandma." I went to her bathroom and picked up the bedpan that I made sure was clean. Wetting a washcloth in warm water and grabbing the Chantilly dusting powder with the pink puff inside, I quickly carried it to her bedside and smiled.

I stood outside her bedroom door until I heard her say, "Okay, sweetie, I'm done."

I returned to her bedside and carefully lifted the bedpan as I balanced it back to the bathroom. I knew to wash it out after flushing and set it on the towel on the floor.

Each time she would thank me with a hug and a kiss.

Even though she may have felt helpless at times, I never witnessed any bitterness from her. Maybe that's why I've never felt resentment for what happened to me.

"Never carry anger in your heart, Linda, it will only cause you pain."

Unfortunately, Grandma was usually in her bed or in her wheelchair. Mama explained to us that Grandma had something called arthritis in her spine, and she could no longer walk without help. I loved to help her balance her feet to move from the bed to her favorite rocking chair.

Grandma was the daughter of a minister. She loved to tell us how she met her husband, our grandfather, who she explained now lived in heaven. She'd played the organ in church, and Grandpa had sung in the choir. He was such a handsome man, and she was so proud of him. He was the chief of police in Hartsville for a long time. He was only in his fifties when he died from cancer. She told us how the police department blew a whistle as a signal to the entire town to close all the stores. Townspeople walked together down the streets to the First Baptist Church of Hartsville on the day of his funeral. He was so loved by everyone in town. He died the year before I was born. How I wished I could have known him too.

My sister and I never noticed Grandma's wheelchair. We only saw her beautiful face with the broad smile that appeared every time we walked into the room. No wonder Grandpa had been drawn to her. She drew everyone in with that angelic face.

Grandma also used Scripture verses to reassure us. I remember her favorite verse was Psalm 56:3, "What time I am afraid, I will trust in Thee" (KJV).

I remembered that Scripture after one terrifying night in particular.

A beautiful guest house was right next to our home, and we used it for family get-togethers. One day we had a family birthday party in the house. We had lots of fun roasting hot dogs in the fireplace.

Later that night, I heard Mama screaming, "Linda, Wanda, come quickly!"

I popped up and yelled, "What's wrong, Mama?" I began to cry.

She came bursting through the door, still wearing only her nightgown, and grabbed both our hands as she rushed us out of the house.

I could see red flames outside my bedroom window as we ran, and I heard people screaming. I could already smell the smoke seeping through the windows as the wind blew hard against the house.

"Mama, what about Grandma?" I pulled on Mama's hand and tried to run toward her bedroom.

"Don't worry about her, sweetie, Daddy already got her out!"

With hot flames burning, the lights of the firetruck lit up the sky. The sirens were so loud we pressed our hands into our ears to protect them. The firemen came rushing out, pulling on a screeching long hose, and sprayed the house. The house melted before our eyes and smoke filled the air.

We were all safe, but frightened. I shivered, holding Grandma close, as we watched the fire go out.

The fire traumatized Wanda and me but this time we had Grandma's lap and loving parents there to console us and promise that they would always protect us.

After the fire, I was afraid to leave Grandma alone. Mama and Daddy had a farm to take care of and they needed to go pick beans, peas, and corn almost every day. Mama thought I just didn't like the hard work in the fields, but Grandma and I knew better.

After everyone left the house, I pulled up my favorite chair, the small straight-backed one with the green seat cushion. Grandma opened the bottom drawer to her nightstand and pulled out boxes of candy to share with me. Next, she reached in another drawer to pull out her Bible and a hymnal. I'd sit for hours listening to her lovely voice singing about God's love for me.

I soaked in the words like a sponge, imagining what God must look like. She even had a picture of Jesus on the wall right over her bed. She'd read to me the words in red in her Bible and explain how much God loved me and brought me into her life.

I cherished the special bond Grandma and I had. I loved watching Billy Graham on TV with her. I'd climb up in her bed beside her and sing all the hymns together. She had a beautiful voice. She could sing either soprano or alto. I loved hearing her harmonize right along with the choir. Before long, I memorized every verse of each song. The words were being etched on my heart.

After Grandma's hands became too swollen with arthritis to write, I helped her write her monthly checks to the Billy Graham Evangelistic Association. It was the only charity she ever supported.

Grandma loved for Wanda and me to spend time with her as she sat in her rocker by the window. Since she could not walk without assistance, I learned how to hold her hand in mine and help her balance from her bed to her rocking chair. I was only about ten years old, but I was determined to help her all by myself. She had her favorite orange and green afghan that we always had to tuck in around her legs to keep her warm. She kept sweet butter mints by her chair and always shared them with me as a thank-you for being willing to help her walk every day.

I didn't find out until much later what my grandmother had gone through in her life. She met her husband while playing the piano in her church and he sang in the choir. My grandfather became the chief of police in their town and they had nine children. She lost one of her sons when he was only three years old to diphtheria. My mother told me a story once about when little Charlie was buried. Grandma made sure he wore his boots because he always wanted to be like his father who wore boots every day as he "walked the beat." Grandma had been an invalid most of her life. Her older children helped take care of the younger ones, as most did in those days. Her children respected and adored their father and mother, and they all became successful men and women in the community. After her beloved husband passed away, Grandma came to live with my mother and father. Five years later, my parents adopted us.

I catch myself many times beginning to panic when storms come into my life. That feeling of insecurity can still haunt me. It's then that I go to a quiet place and let my memory return me to that old rocking chair and I listen to her calm voice assuring me that I am someone special and that I am truly loved. Grandma's quiet, sweet spirit spoke volumes to my heart. She never shouted. She never preached. She just lived out her love for God before me and I learned by her example that I too could trust Him.

girls with grandma

Squirrel Catchin'

Geronimo! We got him!

July 1959
Lydia, South Carolina
Linda

Days in our new home seemed to go by so fast. Each morning's sunrise brought the light of a new day, only to quickly fade away at sunset.

As Mama tucked me into bed one evening, I asked, "What are we going to do tomorrow?"

"Tomorrow? Child, tomorrow you're going to meet your cousin, Danny Ray." She chuckled under her breath. "He's a pistol, that one. I'm sure he will teach you some interesting things."

Mama kissed my forehead and turned out the light.

"A pistol?" I imagined this poor boy, all funny shaped, trying to teach me things.

What on earth could I learn from him? I blinked my eyes a few more times and then drifted off to sleep.

The next morning, the sun peeked through the curtains in my room. The warm light felt good on my face. I jumped up to the sound of someone, a child, running around the house.

Oh, goodness, he's here. I heard him chasing a ball around in the kitchen as his mother yelled at him to take it outside.

"Danny Ray, you best get outside with that ball before I take this spoon to your hide!"

I grabbed my boots and stopped at the kitchen door, taking a deep breath to prepare myself to see this odd-shaped boy. I could still hear the ball bouncing, with the pounding of feet behind it, and still more behind that as his mama chased him through the house.

When I opened the door to see, I was so relieved. Danny Ray was no pistol-shaped boy. He was just as normal as any other boy. I thought he was wild and kind of cute, much like the other boys I'd seen in town.

Danny Ray was a stocky boy with a crew cut. He had dark brown eyes and the cutest smile I've ever seen.

"Oh, hi. Thank heavens you're awake," Mama said as she handed me a hot biscuit filled with grape jelly, not realizing how hot it was in my hands.

"Good morning, Mama," I said, balancing the hot biscuit from one hand to the other.

"Here, take your breakfast, honey, and Danny Ray, too, outside for me quickly, okay?" she whispered.

"Come on now, girl," Danny Ray said while running past, a sly grin on his face. "I got lots of things to show you."

I ran so fast after Danny Ray that I couldn't keep up with my feet.

"Danny Ray, slow down! What are we running for?"

"Run, girl. We got squirrel catchin' to do today."

My eyes lit up. This sounded like an adventure worth getting into.

Danny Ray slid into the bushes, and I followed quickly behind. "See there, girl? I set the trap." I could hear pride in his voice.

I was instantly drawn to Danny Ray. Wanda was, too, though at first, we were so gullible that we believed his every word. I certainly did that first day.

"Danny Ray, what are we catchin'?"

Danny Ray shook his head with disappointment. "Squirrels, I told you!" He shouted, but quickly put his finger over his own mouth as if I was the one who'd spoken too loudly.

"Squirrels?" I crammbed the last bite of biscuit in my mouth. "How do you catch them, and what do you do with them when you do catch them?"

Laughing under his breath, he shook his head. "I put food in that box. Don't you see the string?"

I nodded my head and leaned in close to whisper. "Yes."

"Once they are in the box, I pull the string. The top shuts and they don't know what happened." He snickered.

My mind wandered as I imagined him back at his house with a room full of squirrels. "You done this before, Danny Ray?"

"Uh, no, but if I was a squirrel and saw some food just lying there, I'd eat it. Wouldn't you?"

I thought about this for a moment and realized he was probably right. This had to work.

"What did you put in the box?"

"Your mama's cheese. She just left it out on the counter."

"Squirrels eat cheese?"

"All animals eat cheese, girl." He may have had a point, and I wasn't going to argue.

Danny Ray took a big chunk of Mama's cheese and with gentle steps, placed a little more cheese in the box. He must have forgotten to be quiet because on the way back he slid into the bushes, nearly knocking me down.

"Shhhhh!" he said, placing his finger once again on his lips.

This time, I didn't hesitate, but I rolled my eyes. This boy just might be crazy. Maybe that's what Mama meant by "he's a pistol, that Danny Ray." He was wild!

It seemed like hours went by, and I was just beginning to realize we weren't catching anything.

But Danny Ray didn't take his eyes off that box. He kept twiddling with the string in his fingers, slowly pulling the string to check on its ability to close the box.

Finally, there was a rustling in the woods, and we turned our heads. It was a squirrel! We could hear the crackling of the leaves under the furry critter's toes.

Danny Ray couldn't keep still. He began rocking back and forth as the animal crawled closer.

The squirrel investigated the box with more concern than Danny Ray had planned. After a few looks around, the squirrel took the risk and climbed in the box.

"Geronimo! We got him!" Danny Ray screamed like a girl.

I couldn't believe my eyes. Then, with a giant leap, Danny Ray jumped up in the air and full-on tackled the box, flattening it completely.

"Danny!" I screamed in horror. "What are you going to do with a squashed squirrel?"

Danny Ray jumped to his feet and pulled himself together. "I don't know. I didn't think too much about it. I pulled the string, but the box didn't shut, so I had to think fast."

"I don't think you thought too much at all, considering the mess we're in now. Danny Ray, you gonna look in the box or what?"

I put my hands on my hips in disgust. I could tell Danny Ray didn't like the sight of blood and guts any more than I did.

"*You* do it."

"Nuh-uh, Danny Ray, I'm not the one who decided to flatten that squirrel. Now you better go get that thing."

Danny Ray took a couple of turns around the box, just like that now flattened squirrel did earlier. He crept down on his knees and picked up the corner of the box.

"I can't see a lick." He peered into the box.

"Is it dead?" I put my hands over my eyes.

"Hot darn! That varmint got away!" He sounded more relieved than disappointed.

I decided to take a look for myself. Sure enough, the box was empty.

"He must be the fastest squirrel around."

We laughed as we rolled on the ground.

We heard Mama call from the porch steps, "Linda, Danny Ray! Come on inside. Almost time for dinner."

Danny Ray led the way running, and again I was running so fast I felt my feet lift off the ground.

"You two have been out there all morning. What's got your attention so?"

I looked at Danny Ray and smiled. "We were out there squirrel catchin'."

Mama smirked and looked at Aunt Edith. "What do you plan to do with them once you catch them?"

Danny Ray looked at Mama and then at Aunt Edith.

"Eat 'em," he said with a grin.

"Eww!" I screamed.

"Danny Ray, where on earth have you heard about eating squirrels?" Aunt Edith seemed embarrassed.

"Well, Mama, I haven't eaten one before, but I heard Daddy and Uncle Carwell talking about skinning them and cooking them over the grill. They said it tastes just like chicken, 'cept you don't have to pay for it!"

Mama, Aunt Edith, and I laughed, though I was feeling a bit nauseous, too.

"Go on and get cleaned up. Dinner is almost ready." Mama was still laughing as she turned to the counter looking for her cheese, not knowing it was squirrel bait.

Mama and Aunt Edith worked on the food preparations for the day. It was a big production when family came over. Mama made her famous mac and cheese, collards, ham with rice and gravy, delicious pies, and of course, her yummy fudge. The smells from the kitchen seem to draw in more folks throughout the day, and by dinnertime, we had a feast big enough for the whole town.

After dinner, we joined Wanda for a game of Go Fish on the front porch. I kept staring at Danny Ray. The gap between his front teeth was like a water spigot. You had to weave back and forth to dodge a shot of spit to the eye. He reminded me of someone else I met in my new family—Aunt Lula.

Aunt Lula was married to my Daddy's brother, Uncle Fletcher. I tried to like her, but it was hard. See, Aunt Lula had this strange habit of spitting. I didn't understand why she did this because I was not allowed to spit. She seemed like an outlaw to me.

Mama called it "dipping snuff." I don't think Mama liked her spitting either, especially in front of Wanda and me.

One day a while back, while riding in the back seat of Daddy's car on the way home from our weekly visit, Wanda and I had been pretending we were dipping snuff. We pulled our bottom lip out and put our tongues in front of our teeth and tried to talk.

"Look, Wanda, I see cows." I tried to say with my two fingers in front of my mouth as spit dribbled down my chin. I couldn't stop laughing, and Wanda was in hysterics.

"What are you girls doing back there?" Mama laughed as she turned around in her seat.

"Dippin' snuff." Wanda giggled.

I saw Mama and Daddy look at each other and smile.

When we'd gotten home, Wanda and I found Mama's cocoa, which she'd left out from making us chocolate milk that morning.

"This looks like snuff, don't you think, Wanda?" I whispered.

She nodded her head and smiled.

We took the cocoa outside and copied what Aunt Lula had done.

"Pull your lip down, Wanda, like this." I showed her how to pull out her lip and put a pinch of cocoa in her mouth.

Wanda copied me as I explained the process and we both smiled a crooked brown smile.

"Okay, Wanda, now take these two fingers and spit between them."

We took our index finger and our middle finger and tried to spit on the ground. We both kept spitting until all the cocoa in our mouths was gone. We could hardly spit for laughing so much. Our shoes were splattered with brown sludge. I looked at Wanda, whose face was streaked with brown slime and fingerprints. I pointed to her, and she pointed to me, and we laughed until we fell down.

Wanda decided to pick up the cocoa can and get some more. She buried her face in the can and took a big sniff.

That was the wrong thing to do. It was like a big bomb had gone off as a cloud of chocolate powder suddenly flew out of the can. Wanda dropped the can and began to choke. Her rasp sounded like a bullfrog croaking.

I ran inside. "Mama, come quick! Wanda is choking! She's gonna die!"

I stood there in complete shock, thinking for sure I was watching my sister's last moments on this earth.

Mama dashed outside, the screen door slamming shut behind her.

Wanda was still coughing when Mama got there. Her hair was a mess, and her tiny face was covered in spit and chocolate.

"She is a sight for sore eyes," Mama said, shaking her head. I didn't know what that meant, but she just patted Wanda on the back and brought her a drink of water. "Now, now, child, you'll be all right."

With Mama's magic touch, Wanda stopped choking, to my great relief.

I saw Mama look around, then right at Wanda and me.

"Girls, what on earth did you get into?"

Then she noticed the can of cocoa on the ground.

I bowed my head in shame. "Well, Mama, we were pretending to dip snuff, like Aunt Lula."

I wanted to sneak back inside behind that loud screen door and hide.

Mama just sighed. "Oh, I see. Well, it looks like you both got your own punishment."

Mama put the can of cocoa high up in the cabinet. That was the last time we tried the nasty habit of "dipping snuff."

Now, staring at Danny Ray over the cards in my hand, I blinked, remembering Aunt Lula and snuff and all we'd been through.

Just then, the sound of Mama's panicked voice brought my attention back.

"I know I put it right here, Edith!"

The three of us continued to play cards, but I heard Mama and Aunt Edith arguing in the kitchen.

"Well, Frances, I didn't eat it. Maybe you've lost your wits."

Mama called out to the porch. "Linda and Danny Ray, have you seen the block of cheese I had out on the counter to make the macaroni and cheese?"

I gasped. Our heads snapped as we looked at each other with wide eyes.

I was really mad now that I realized Danny Ray used all the cheese trying to catch a stupid squirrel, and I was not going to have my favorite mac and cheese for dinner.

"Go Fish!" Danny Ray shouted, trying to avert my attention and look innocent.

We played for a couple more minutes when I noticed Wanda hadn't looked at her cards. She was off, staring into the distance in some kind of trance.

I tried to look over her shoulder in her direction to see what her eyes were fixed on, but I couldn't see what was so mesmerizing.

"Wanda, what do you see?"

Wanda was still not too good with her words, but suddenly she stood up and shouted with glee.

"Look, Finn! Squirrel, eatin' cheese!"

Linda, Wanda, Danny Ray

No Spitting Allowed

Well I certainly wouldn't tolerate that behavior.

Fond Memories of Our Childhood
Linda

"Come on in here, Linda." I heard Mama call from the kitchen. Mama had made me a blue dotted swiss dress with an oversized silky bow that she neatly tied across the back.

"You made me a new dress?" My eyes grew big as saucers.

"Yes, this is for your birthday party. Now stand still so I can tie the bow just right. You're six years old, and I've planned a party with all your cousins and friends.

"My first birthday party ever." I smiled and saw Mama wipe a tear from her eye.

I wore a full crinoline slip underneath that crunched as I twirled around.

"I feel like a princess, Mama. Thank you. Thank you."

"I made Wanda a dress, just like yours, except her dress is red. Let's put on your black patent leather shoes and frilly white socks to match."

There were balloons of every size, from big white ones to all shades of blue. It looked like clouds floating above a long table filled with gifts.

"Happy Birthday, Linda," everyone said to me. They were wearing funny pointed hats and blowing whistles.

"Thank you so much!" I put my hands to my face, starting to cry.

"Happy Birthday, Finn." Wanda squeezed me tight and held my hand. I stopped crying.

"Thank you, Sissy, you look so pretty."

Since I had been going to Sunday school for a few months, all my classmates came to my party. I was excited to see my cousins as they came running to hug me with gifts in hand. We had fun playing games and running around the yard.

Leon, Daddy's nephew, wore a red and white striped button-down shirt and khaki shorts.

"Hi, Leon," I said. "Thank you for coming to my party."

"You're welcome," he smiled.

"Hi, Kay, I love your dress too."

"Thanks, Linda, my mom just bought it for me to come to your party."

"I hope you don't get it dirty."

"I know. Mama would have a fit." She twisted her white linen dress around and giggled.

There was only one problem at this party, and that was Billy. I made sure I avoided him.

"Danny Ray, Rebecca, let's go play on the swings." I grabbed Danny Ray's hand and gave Billy a look like he better not come with us.

"He's just a bully," I told Danny Ray. "I wish he wasn't at my party."

"Come on, Linda, let's go. Don't worry about him. It's your birthday."

We ran to the swing set, and a bunch of other kids followed.

"Carol, Denise, watch me. Daddy taught me how to pump my legs yesterday," I got higher and higher. "Look at me." I could feel the wind whooshing through my legs. I jumped. I felt like I was flying, just for a moment, before landing on the soft grass.

"Hey Linda, don't look now, but Billy is running over," Danny Ray said.

I took to my feet, running with all my might.

"Stop chasing me!" I yelled as I ran away from him.

Daddy shouted, "Everyone gather around the table. It's time to sing." Thank goodness! I was saved.

I joined all the guests in their silly hats and saw the screen door open. Wearing a beautiful floral sundress, Mama was carrying a white layered cake with blue piped frosting dancing around the edges. She sheltered six candles from the spring breeze as she carried the cake to meet me. Friends and family all singing "Happy Birthday." Daddy was taking pictures, and Bubba was chewing on tennis shoes left on the ground. Mama placed the cake right in front of me.

"All right, Linda, blow the candles out," she said.

I took a deep breath. This would be the first time I ever blew out candles, and I wanted to get all six of them in one try. I filled my lungs, put my lips together, and just when I was about to take that big moment of air, I felt something.

"Billy, stop!" I turned around, and he had untied Mama's perfect bow. I felt tears welling up. Mama came rushing over. "Don't worry, dear, I can fix it," she said. She tied it back just like before, and I took a moment to compose. Smiling but full of rage. I took another breath. Counting just before I released the next breath of air. Then it happened again. Billy, with a nasty smirk on his face, untied it. This time there was no calming me down.

"That's it!" I exclaimed. I turned around, looked directly at him, and said, "I'm gonna get you!" He ran, and I chased him. I embodied all my anger in that moment. I was ready to take him down and make him pay. We ran around the table, each trying not to fall down. Cups were flying off the table, and birthday dresses caught in the wind, but I was determined to catch him. I stopped and turned around. I put my hands on my hips and filled my mouth with as much saliva as I could muster. When that boy came running around the corner, I spit right in his face.

Everyone gasped and stood still, anticipating what would happen next. Mama came running over to me.

"Linda, we don't spit at people!" She reprimanded. "Tell Billy you're sorry right now!"

"But, Mama, he untied my bow."

Holding back her giggles, she turned to Billy and cleaned his face with a napkin.

"Billy, we don't chase the girls and untie their bows, okay?" she scolded.

"Well I certainly wouldn't tolerate that behavior," someone said. Mama turned her head to see where those remarks came from, but she ignored them.

As the sun set and everyone left the party, I sat alone on the back porch steps. Daddy saw me sitting there and came to join me.

"You've had a big day, haven't you?" I felt his arm pull me in close to him.

"Yes, sir. I think this has been the best day of my life, except for Billy."

Daddy laughed. "Boys, huh? One day you'll change your mind."

"I don't think so."

"Some boys are bullies, but there are some others who are nice."

I agreed.

"You might not understand it now, but when boys chase you, it usually means they like you. They just don't know the right way to show it. They'll learn one day. Tomorrow is another day with lots of new adventures. Let's call Freckles and give her hay before bedtime, okay?"

I jumped up and gave him a big hug. We skipped, hand in hand, toward the barn, calling the cows and laughing.

JUL • 59 Linda turns 6!

Linda's birthday party 1959

No More Pancakes

Come on Wanda. Come on Linda. make enough butter,
so we'll all have some!

Spring, 1960
Linda

I loved our home in the country. We had a huge yard, a swing set, and a sandbox to build our sandcastles. Bubba, our wonderful Australian Shepherd, was always nearby, ready to protect us as we played. Daddy owned many black and white dairy cows who were always watching us from the other side of the fence.

One day I noticed a cow looking at me with her head over the barbed wire fence. It seemed she was not afraid for me to touch her, so I stroked her face and talked softly to her.

"You know, we have something special in common. You have freckles on your pink nose, just like me. I think I'll name you Freckles."

Every day I walked to the fence and waited for her. As soon as she saw me, she waddled her way to the fence, nodding her head up and down and softly responding, "Moo-o-o" to everything I said. We became very close. I knew Freckles was there to listen if I had a bad day.

I made friends with all the animals on the farm—except the mules. Their loud "honking" frightened me. Daddy didn't seem to be afraid of them. He walked up each day, put a set of blinders on them, and plowed the fields. I asked him one day why they had to wear "sun-shades," and he told me the blinders kept them from being distracted or frightened by anything else in the field. That helped the mules look straight ahead and get the fields plowed faster.

"I'm afraid of the donkeys, Daddy. They honk so loudly like they are going to eat me."

"That's their way of talking to you. I promise they won't hurt you. Do you trust me?"

"Sure, Daddy," I smiled and took his hand.

"Okay then, hold this rope." He carefully and slowly put the rope around the donkey's neck and handed me one end of the rope.

When Daddy first handed me the rope, I stared at it and quickly threw it to the ground. It was a thick, braided rope. I shook my head and tried to erase the memory of the ropes around my ankles that con-fused my mind. I picked up the rope and smiled at Daddy, neither of us understanding what had just happened.

"Walk around the fence and lead him. You must show him you're the boss, but you won't hurt him. Once he trusts you, he will obey you. See, he's harmless."

"Okay, Daddy, whatever you say. I'll walk with him, but I still don't like him honking at me."

There were lots of chores to be done on the farm. My favorite thing was to make butter.

"Come into the kitchen, girls," I heard Mama calling early one morning. "I've got a fun project for you."

I looked to see on the counter rows of mason jars turned upside-down in perfectly straight lines on kitchen towels. Mama obviously had spent a long time washing the jars. On the floor next to the table was a large, wooden jug with a stick in it.

"What's that?" I blinked several times in confusion.

"That's the butter churn. Here, I'll show you how it works. After we milk the cows, we leave the buckets undisturbed, allowing the cream to rise to the top. I then skim the cream off the top each morning. That's what we use to make the butter. Then I put the cream in the churn and plunge the dasher, or stick, up and down. It takes about thirty minutes of plunging to cause the fat in the cream to form small clumps of butter. I pour off the rest of the buttermilk for biscuits, put the churned butter in a bowl, and then rinse with cold water. Next, I take this butter paddle and knead the butter to make it smooth. I add a touch of salt for flavor. Then I put the butter in the jars and store them in the refrigerator.

"Can I keep my jar and put my name on it?" I asked Mama.

"Sure, you can." She grinned and winked at Nina, our nanny and Mama's helper in the kitchen.

Plunging the churn was too hard for Wanda and me, so Mama and Nina poured some of the cream into the mason jars for us to shake.

"Hop up here on the stools, and I'll let you make some butter too. Here's a jar for you, Linda, and one for you too, Wanda."

Nina taught us a silly song her mother had taught her about churning butter.

> *Peter's at the gate, waiting for the butter cake,*
>
> *Come butter come, come butter come,*
>
> *Peter's at the gate, waiting for the butter cake,*

Come butter come, Come butter come,

Come on, Wanda, Come on, Linda,

Make enough butter, so we'll all have some!"

Peter's at the gate, waiting for the butter cake,

Come butter come, Come butter, come!

We hopped down from the bar stools, jumped up and down in the kitchen, shaking our jars and giggling so hard we almost wet our clothes!

There was always laughter in Mama's kitchen while doing daily chores. Our home out in the country was a very busy place—people coming and going all the time. I was so excited the day I met Nina. That's what Wanda and I called her because we couldn't say her full name, Evelina. She lived near the farm and was one of Mama and Daddy's biggest helpers.

Nina informed me that she would come every morning to fix breakfast for us.

"I heard your favorite breakfast is pancakes. Is that right, Linda?" Nina grinned.

I nodded my head and smiled.

One morning I had already had two helpings of pancakes, but I begged for a third.

"Don't you give that child any more pancakes," Mama insisted.

"Aw, but ma'am, the child's still hungry."

"Okay, Nina, if she insists, go ahead and give her another helping, but I guarantee she won't keep them down." I wondered how it was that Mama always knew what would happen to me before I did.

Nina loved Wanda and me like we were her own. She cooked the best breakfasts and lunches. I remember her always wearing white dresses with pretty aprons over them.

Nina took her time combing and clipping barrettes behind our ears. You would have thought Wanda and I were twins by the way our dresses matched and our hairstyles were identical.

We had so much fun visiting Nina at her home. She showed us how to bake cookies and make banana nut bread.

"I never knew squishing bananas could be so much fun." I giggled.

I remember chasing the chickens and laughing at the tiny piglets squealing in her backyard. It was like going to a petting zoo when we stayed with Nina.

Visiting Nina

Snakes in the Sandbox

My mama chose me. Your mama had to keep you!

August 1960
Linda

The smell of bacon frying in the kitchen woke me up one morning.

"Good morning, sleepyheads." Mama smiled at us as she looked back from her frying pan. "I'm making a good breakfast for you, Linda, before you catch the bus for your first day at school. Aren't you excited?"

"I guess so. Do I really have to go?"

"Yes, you do, and I know you'll have so much fun." Mama tried to sound convincing.

Starting first grade was a scary day for me. It was even more traumatizing for Wanda, who had to stay home.

Our driveway was very long. Nina helped with cleaning the kitchen while Mama carried Wanda and held my hand as we made the long walk to catch the big yellow school bus.

I climbed up the steps and looked back, hoping Mama would change her mind. I then noticed my best friend, Elizabeth, motioning for me to sit on the seat beside her by the window.

"Bye, bye," Mama called out several times, waving goodbye as I stared out the bus window, my little hand waving as I held in my tears. Mama tried to walk fast back to the house so that I wouldn't notice Wanda kicking and screaming for me, but I did notice.

"Bye, Sissy!" I yelled out the window as the bus sped away.

Thankfully, we'd had a few months to settle into our home on the farm before we were separated yet again. But this time, it was only for a short time during the day at school, and I got to come back to my safe place after only a few hours.

Mama sat me down one day to explain what adoption meant. She'd wanted me to be prepared when I went to school in case someone said something to me about being adopted. And sure enough, when I got to school, a boy made a remark about my being adopted.

Michael ran up to me on the playground before all my new friends and said, "My mama told me that you're adopted!"

I quickly put my hands on my hips and responded, "Yep, my mama chose me. Your mama had to keep you!"

Mama said she was very proud that I felt so special about being adopted.

"But always know that you are not my adopted daughters—you are my daughters, period."

In her innocent little mind, Wanda somewhat understood what being adopted was too.

"I bet you wish you were adopted, Ricky," she'd said to her new friend at church.

"Why?" he asked.

"Well, because if you were adopted, you'd have a bathroom inside your house."

I had only one major problem with school. I did get to ride a big, bright-yellow school bus each day, which was lots of fun. But, when I got off the bus in the afternoon, I had to walk down the long driveway to the house, which meant I had to walk past the mules. Their honking scared me to tears.

Late one afternoon, Mama asked, "Nina, what time is it?"

"It's after 3:00 p.m.," Nina said with worry in her voice.

"Linda should have made it to the house by now. Would you please walk down and see if she got off the bus?"

Without hesitation, Nina began the long walk down the driveway.

She found me still sitting at the end of the driveway, refusing to take another step. One of the mules had his head through the wire and honked at me every time I made a move.

I jumped up and ran to Nina, thankful she had saved my life.

Living out in the country had great rewards. We loved riding our bikes in our shorts and bare feet through the long country dirt roads from one friend's home to another. I was getting so good at riding my bicycle that I could balance it with no hands for miles down the road. My bike riding didn't start out that way, though. Somehow, Wanda had managed to jump on her bike the first few times and ride away. I wasn't quite so secure with mine, and I jumped off each time the front wheel started to weave back and forth.

One of Daddy's farmhands, Dewey, felt sorry for me. He was also the church custodian and Nina's husband. Dewey came over one day and worked with me for a long time until I could balance my bike without falling off. Wanda was proud that she had learned something new before I did. But once I got it, there was no turning back. The only fear we had riding our bikes in the country was watching out for snakes.

Late one afternoon, I heard Mama scream at the top of her lungs. "Carwell, Carwell, come quick!"

Daddy jumped up from the couch and ran into the kitchen.

"What's the matter, Frances?"

"Look out the window. There's a huge snake crawling across the children's sandbox!"

Daddy grabbed the phone and called Dewey.

"Drive the tractor with the lift attached over here quick, Dewey, and bring a gun and a shovel!" Daddy shouted.

"Bang, bang, bang." Three shots echoed through the bamboo forest.

After killing the snake, they hoisted it up and measured it. I was told it was over eight feet long and about a foot thick. Dewey hauled the giant snake to the pond nearby. We named the pond "The Black Lagoon," and we never went near it again.

Not long after that, the house was on the market for sale.

Mama and Daddy bought an acre of land down the road next to the pastor on Highway 15, in open farmland with hardly any trees. Mama designed her dream home, and Daddy had it built for her. I remember Daddy planted pine trees in the yard. The trees were so small I made a game of jumping over them. One thing was for sure—and much to Mama's relief—there were no more giant snakes.

But there was a railroad track. Right behind our house was a bean field. A few hundred yards away, we could hear the whistle of the train in the distance. Every day we listened for that whistle.

"Finn, Finn—train!" Wanda would call as she ran to get me.

I'd grab Wanda's hand, and we'd go running outside. We jumped over the beans in the field because Daddy had warned us not to step on the farmer's beans. The hot sand burned the bottom of our feet like stinging bees.

The conductor was driving the first car, the big black engine. He proudly wore his overalls and his conductor's striped hat. We'd count the cars: one, two, three, four. We kept counting until we saw the last car—the red caboose. Another man was riding on the back of the caboose. His red hat matched the train car. He'd always wave goodbye to us and would wave until he was out of sight.

It made our day to see the train. We began to think it might have made their day, too, to see us holding hands, laughing and waving at them like we were their friends.

#

Living in our new house had lots of rewards. We also met new neighbors. The preacher at our church, Mt. Elon Baptist Church, lived next door with his wife and three sons. There was a field between the two houses, so we soon made a permanent path between them.

Reverend Thomas Faucette was the name of our wonderful pastor. I listened carefully to what he said every Sunday. His voice was smooth and warm, like honey. Grandma had already told me and read much of what he said in the Scriptures. I looked up to him and trusted his every word. He was a tall man in stature, sincere, wise, and godly. Each of his sermons touched my heart and made a big impression. I knew it was no accident that they were our next-door neighbors.

Ms. Virginia, his wife, became Mama's best friend. They loved to share recipes with each other. We made many trips back and forth through that field as we carried food from the garden, or dishes prepared for them and us.

Wanda and I loved to ride our bikes next door to play with the boys, Jimmy, Stephen and David.

"Stop! State Trooper Highway Patrol!" Jimmy would yell, his hand up in front of us. He'd give us a tongue-lashing for speeding, and we'd get tickets (leaves) for our infraction.

"Boys will be boys," I heard my daddy say many times.

One day, after Christmas, Jimmy brought his new BB gun to show Wanda and me. We had never been around guns, but we were curious.

Wanda decided to look down the barrel of the gun. Just then, her finger slipped—and pulled the trigger.

The loud pow of the gun scared me silly.

"Mama! Wanda is bleeding!" I ran as fast as I could to the house as blood streamed down Wanda's face.

Thankfully, there were no BBs in the gun, but the air pressure caused her nose to bleed. After a harsh punishment, the boys knew guns were never allowed in our presence again.

They were typical boys who thought they were superior to girls. They had received an invitation to Wanda's birthday party one time.

"I'm not going to carry it—you carry it," said Stephen.

"I'm not going to carry it." Jimmy threw the package back to Stephen. Mrs. Faucette called Mama on the phone as she watched the boys out the window on their way to our house for a birthday party.

"I'm sorry, Frances, I'm not sure what shape the gift will be in when it arrives. The boys are tossing it back and forth all the way over there. Neither one wants to show up with a doll!" They both laughed out loud.

For some reason, almost every time we played with the boys, we got into some kind of trouble. Wanda always copied everything we did. I loved to swing upside down on the swing set monkey bars. She tried and tried to stay on the bar, too.

One day she fell straight down—and began to cry.

"Mama, Wanda is hurt!" I cried out, fetching Mama once again.

We rushed to the doctor to find out she had broken her collarbone. I felt terrible. I waited on her hand and foot until the sling was removed a few weeks later.

From the time I was very young, I always felt responsible for taking care of my baby sister. That motherly instinct stayed with me throughout my life.

Neighborhood gang at the pool

Baptism Day

Buried with Christ in baptism—raised to walk in newness of life.

July 9, 1962
Linda

Listening to Reverend Faucette each Sunday was the highlight of my week. One Sunday, July 9, 1962, I walked down the aisle as the congregation sang "I Surrender All." I told Reverend Faucette that I had accepted Jesus in my heart and wanted to follow Him all my life.

Mrs. Faucette, my Girls in Action teacher, told me about missions. I had the desire and vision in my heart to be a missionary when I grew up. Mrs. Faucette made the Scriptures come alive for me in the way she explained them. All we girls in GAs had to memorize Scriptures every week in order to get rewards. We even had to appear before the "review board," a group of older ladies in the church who made sure we memorized them correctly. We had a special day of recognition. It was called a coronation. I cried the day of my coronation because Mama had given me a curly permanent, and I hated it.

Our day of baptism was a memorable event. Wanda and I were baptized together on Sunday, July 16, 1962.

Mama made us matching white dresses for our special day. Mine had buttons all the way down the front. We had to wait in the small bathroom in the back of the church and then walk out into the baptismal pool.

Reverend Faucette asked Wanda and me each if we had made the decision to accept Jesus into our hearts. We both assured him we had. I'll never forget his beautiful words: "I baptize you, my sister in Christ, in the name of the Father, the Son, and the Holy Spirit. Buried with Christ in baptism, raised to walk in newness of life."

I cried because I felt unworthy of God's love and forgiveness, yet I was happy to have the assurance that I was His child forever. I had a new earthly father and a heavenly Father, too.

The next step in my life and my walk with Jesus was attending GA (Girl's Auxiliary) Camp. This was my first time away from home overnight. I had spent a night or two with my relatives at pajama parties, but never had I spent an entire week away from the security of my new home.

At GA Camp, I loved the cabins and all my new friends. Several of my friends from church were with me, as well as Mrs. Faucette, so I was not totally alone. I really loved my cabin counselor, who made a big impression on me when she insisted on nightly devotions and prayers. I was not much of a morning person, so I didn't like getting up early to shower, but I did love to eat, so I always made it up in time for breakfast.

We were so lucky to have a big lake to swim in, and our evenings were spent playing games and singing songs. The last night at camp, we all got in a long line all around the campfire. We held candles and sang songs. "We've a Story to Tell to the Nations" was our theme song. It was a beautiful sight to see.

I was happy to go to camp but even happier to go home. When Mama and Daddy came on the last day to pick me up, I started to cry.

"Usually, children cry when their parents leave them, not when they come to get them," Mama said as she hugged my neck.

But she soon realized why I was crying. She was my security. While I'd had fun at camp, the fear of abandonment still haunted me. I was so relieved to see them, not only because I'd missed them, but because I realized I'd not been abandoned again. They had come back for me, just like they promised.

Mama could tell from this experience that I depended on her a lot. She worked daily to instill high values and morals and love for others by example. I looked at her face sometimes and wondered if I'd have the same kind of love she had, to accept two sad little girls into her life. She had to start over with us like we were babies. We were babies when she got us in the sense that we had to learn what love really was. We had to learn what trust was. We learned it through Mama and Daddy's unconditional love toward us.

I've heard it said that children's personalities are set by the time they are three years old. I believe that environment, maybe even more than genetics, determines our personalities. Wanda and I would have been far different people if we'd been left in those foster homes or orphanages. We have different personalities today because of the loving environment we were fortunate enough to be given by God's own hand.

Swimming Lessons

I decided I didn't like swimming lessons.

Lawton Park
Summer of 1963
Linda

"Good morning, my sweet girl. Did you have sweet dreams?" Mama winked at me as I slowly strolled down the hall, still in my pink pajamas, being awakened by the smells wafting from the kitchen.

I am not a morning person, so I didn't answer right away. I crawled up in the chair and grabbed a warm, sweet biscuit. With my mouth full, my eyes brightened, "Mama, you're the best cook in the whole wide world."

She stroked my hair out of my eyes and smiled. Mama had waited many years to have a little girl sitting at her table. She turned away and wiped the tears from her cheeks with her dishcloth. After she regained her composure, she turned back around and smiled.

"As soon as you finish breakfast, go wake up Wanda. We are going to the park to play today."

I loved Lawton Park. Wanda and I swung, climbed on the monkey bars, and spun around until we were dizzy on the merry-go-round. It's one of the best parks in town and we always found many friends there waiting to play with us.

When summer arrived, Mama brought out our new swimsuits. I loved my one-piece with bright, beautiful flowers all over it. Wanda's was so cute with yellow ruffles all the way around, like a skirt.

"This summer, girls, you are going to take swimming lessons at Lawton Park," Mama announced with a big smile on her face. "It's important that you learn how to swim. You go to Elizabeth's pool a lot and some of your cousins have pools, so your daddy and I want to be sure you learn how to swim correctly."

"That sounds like fun." Wanda and I quickly put on our swimsuits.

I loved my swim teacher. She was so nice and kind as she instructed us on how to hold our breath and swim underwater. Somehow, Wanda caught on quickly and followed each direction precisely. I was used to Elizabeth's pool where I could see all the way to the bottom. I could see where my feet were, and there was clean, clear water in the pool. Not so in the lake at Lawton Park. I couldn't see my feet and I felt icky stuff on the bottom. I decided I didn't like swimming lessons.

We had to go to the lake every day for a whole week. Somehow, I made it through until Friday. It was finally graduation day. Our final test was to jump off the end of the pier into the deep, muddy water and swim to the instructor. Little Wanda ran down the plank with no fear and jumped into the arms of our instructor. But when it was my turn, I would not be getting my certificate of accomplishment for swimming lessons that day. I walked slowly down the dock, crying all the way. When I reached the end, the instructor said, "Jump, Linda! I'll catch you and then you can swim back to the dock."

The water seemed darker than ever to me. I refused to jump, turned around, and ran back to Mama. I can't see the bottom, Mama!" I screamed.

"That's okay, honey, you've done a good job all week learning to swim. I suppose you can learn diving in the clear pool at Elizabeth's."

"Thank goodness. I promise I will."

To this day I will not swim in the lake.

Some of my fondest memories are the days Wanda and I spent swimming in Elizabeth's pool. We were lucky our best friend had a pool in her backyard. Her dad had decided that one way to keep his children close was to install a swimming pool. All the kids in the neighborhood met at Elizabeth's every day during the summer and swam for hours. Elizabeth was a much better teacher for me to learn how to swim. She taught me how to dive and swim in deep water.

We loved meeting all our friends there during the summer months. The older children would teach the younger ones to swim. The Faucette boys always came over too from next door, and Elizabeth, being the oldest child there, would patiently teach them how to swim. We all looked out for each other, and her parents were always nearby, keeping a watchful eye.

I'm sure my swim coach at the lake was a good teacher, but my trust issues from my experiences during early childhood caused me to struggle with trusting people I did not know. I had to learn to trust myself as well as others. I am still very cautious around new people I meet. I am very discerning and recognize fake people right away. It took years for me to let go of the negative things that I went through as a child and begin to trust the people who loved me.

Mama Pearl & Runaway Cows

I meet with him again each time and have peace with it.

Spring, 1965
Linda

"A in't you ever been married before?" I asked Mama Pearl as we sat side by side on her porch swing.

I had no idea what a question like that would mean to a sweet, elderly lady. I was twelve years old that spring, and since my grandmother had passed away suddenly from a stroke the summer before, my heart ached from missing her so much.

I had become very close to our next-door neighbor, whom we all affectionately called "Mama Pearl." Her soft, gray hair was pinned back, framing her neck and face. I could see it must be long, but she always had it neatly rolled up with bobby pins. She didn't seem to mind the wispy hairs that blew softly by her eyes and cheeks. Her eyes always reminded me of a clear, blue river—a blue that would wrap around and carry you away.

Mama Pearl stared off into the distance, looking deeply beyond the pastures across the road.

"Mama Pearl, did I say something wrong?"

"No, dear. I'm just trying to decide how to tell you."

"Tell me what?"

"You see those cows over there, far into the pasture?"

"Yes, ma'am."

"Well, each time I walk over there, I pet them. I talk to them and remember my husband."

"Why do you do that? What happened to him?"

"Linda, next month, will mark exactly thirty years since the day my life changed forever."

As Mama Pearl told me her story, we rocked back and forth on the warm summer day.

"Spring was leaving us with the thick heat of summer creeping in. That night the breeze through our windows was strong, and we were sleeping hard. We had worked all day in the fields. We were plumb tuckered out."

She laughed as she shook her head. She placed her hand on my knee as we continued to rock in the wind. I could tell it was getting harder for her to speak.

She took a long breath and continued.

"Back then, farmers worked early hours before the hot sun rose each day and before some of them had to go to work at their main jobs. It was 5:15 a.m. when we heard the horns blowing and the horrible noises that followed. Linda, I can still hear it as loudly as that morning. I'll never forget it."

I stopped swinging and listened.

"We both jumped up out of bed," Mama Pearl continued. "Robert was stumbling to get his clothes on. Poor man had just enough time to get in his overalls. He didn't even get his boots on the right feet. But there was no time to stop, no time for me to help him get out the door. It all happened so fast. Before I knew it, he was gone. I was getting my robe on when I heard the door slam. In the chaos, Robert must have pushed my slippers under the bed, or maybe I did, as I was so frantic too, but just in that moment, as I was searching for them, I heard it."

I leaned in close to her and asked, "Heard what, Mama Pearl?"

"Oh, Linda, it was just awful. The cows had gotten out of the field and were stampeding across the main road. Cars were swerving and the big eighteen-wheelers were laying on their horns. Trying to save those animals, Robert ran out there. They were our livelihood. It was the only way we survived each year, with what little we had. Out there in his boots, overalls, and an unbuttoned shirt, he waved his arms for the cars to stop.

But it was just turning daylight, and that man didn't see him. The cows had kicked up the dust so badly. No one could see a thing. The man's name was Bill. On his way to work in town, he drove in every morning past our house. His truck was gray and blended in with the dust.

"He hit Robert straight on. Bill thought he had hit one of the cows in the cluttered mess and dust that morning. But my scream from the front porch, as I was running out, made him realize what he had done."

I gasped and put my hand over my mouth. She held my other hand so tightly I could only see white in my veins.

"Screaming and crying, I ran over to Robert. The neighbors had all come out and were running around chasing the cows to get them back in the fence. Your daddy was out there, too, helping them round up the cattle."

Without saying anything, I smiled at the thought of my daddy being there.

"There was so much dust and rocks flying around it was hard to see anything. When I got to Robert, he was so badly broken that he hadn't much left in him. I knelt down, placed his head in my hands, and watched his eyes fade into the light of the Lord."

Mama Pearl looked deep into my eyes. "Linda, he loved God so much that I know he felt no pain when he got hit. The Lord just carried him away. That's why I go out to the fields, pet the cows, and talk to them. I meet with him again each time and have peace with it."

Still grieving the loss of her sweet husband, tears flowed like the river from Mama Pearl's eyes. She took the handkerchief she always kept neatly tucked under her watch and wiped her tears.

I lifted my T-shirt and wiped my own eyes. We sat silently for a long time as I put my arm around her and swung back and forth on the porch.

The bond between us grew deeper from that moment.

After Grandma passed away, Mama found it necessary and good therapy for her to return to work. Wanda and I had no problem with Mama returning to work, because as soon as we jumped off the bus, we walked next door with our friend, Elizabeth, or as I called her, Idgie, and stayed with her all afternoon.

Mama Pearl was Idgie's grandmother. She often asked us what we wanted to do with our lives growing up. She was so easy to talk to and always had good advice when we needed it. She was genuinely interested in us because she felt we were so special. Idgie was my best friend. She, too, was an adopted child. That gave us all a special kindred spirit and made Mama Pearl cherish us so much.

Idgie was two years older than I was and so smart. She was tall for her age and had a big smile. I always admired her long, flowing brown hair. We had so much fun rolling our hair on huge curlers the size of orange juice cans. She'd gladly assist me with my math homework. Math was my worst subject, but it came so naturally to her. In high school, we both loved writing in shorthand. We found it funny to write to each other in shorthand silly things about the boys on the bus because we knew they couldn't read our notes.

"How great thou art," I'd hear Mama Pearl singing along with George Beverley Shea as I came in the back door after school. Another one of her favorite albums was Elvis singing gospel songs.

I loved listening to this sweet Christian lady. She was always happy despite the sad things that had happened in her lifetime. Many things I never knew about until years later.

Mama Pearl never did get her driver's license, so Idgie would pick her up each Sunday and take her to church. Mama Pearl once won the title "Mother of the Year." Deservedly so. Unfortunately, Mama Pearl also lost her fifteen-year-old daughter, Dorothy, to leukemia sometime after she lost her husband. Idgie and I always admired Mama Pearl and considered her a very strong, independent person, considering all the tragedies she endured. After her husband died, she started working at the Lydia School cafeteria.

Window air conditioners were the new way to cool homes, but Mama Pearl used window fans to keep her house cool in the hot summer months. She did not like the idea of the new contraptions. She preferred raising her windows and opening her hall doors for a breeze that was somehow always cool. Idgie's daddy, Mama Pearl's son, put an air conditioner in a window near her kitchen, but she did not like having to keep her windows and doors shut, so he had to take it back out.

Mama Pearl was also an excellent seamstress. She sewed many of our clothes. I enjoyed watching her with her old sewing machine with the pumping pedal as she feverishly worked away in front of her favorite window. I was always amazed at the finished product she was able to create. I also loved the sweet smells as I came into her home. Mama Pearl was always baking something. She had a snack ready every day for us when we got home from school.

As little girls, Idgie, Wanda, and I loved to sit under Mama Pearl's huge oak tree that covered her driveway like an umbrella. We loved the cool breezes that came through as we sat under it, enjoying our freshly baked brownies and hot chocolate, for which she was so famous. We laughed at our silly drawings and games that we played in the dirt.

Hours flew by quickly as we played hopscotch and jump rope while Mama Pearl watched us from her window. Her driveway wrapped all the way around her house, so we all enjoyed racing our bikes round and round, waving at her each time we passed. The hum of the sewing machine was a welcome sound. We knew her kind, watchful eyes always ensured her special girls were safe.

Mama Pearl's two-story house was full of mysteries and new adventures. Idgie, Wanda, and I were so excited when we asked Mama Pearl for permission to play upstairs. She had a collection of old spools she just couldn't seem to part with, and it seemed there was always a new litter of sweet little kittens coming out from under her house every few months. All three of us girls loved kittens. We each got to pick our special one and brought it inside to tame it. Minutes would turn into hours as we rolled the spools across the floor and giggled as we watched the kittens run back and forth trying to catch the spools. We'd take string and pull it through the spools so the little kittens could play with them all afternoon. After a while, we and the kittens grew tired and snuggled up on one of the old iron beds for an afternoon nap.

It's funny how something as simple as used spools of thread can bring so much entertainment to children. We decorated them with paint and buttons as we strung them around our necks. Mama Pearl was a very frugal person. She never threw anything away that she thought could have another use later. Looking back, I wonder if she saved them because of her wisdom that little things like spools would entertain children.

We loved her beautiful hats and scarves. My favorite scarf was the hot pink chicken-feather boa. Idgie loved the one with yellow ostrich feathers. We laughed at each other as we threw the scarves around our necks and spit out the feathers that stuck to our lips. Mama Pearl had a box of old high-heeled shoes that we took turns trying on. After we were all dressed up, we'd put on a fashion show for her. I still remember that sweet smile as she laughed at us silly little girls prancing down the long, hardwood floor in the hall in our fancy attire like we were on a runway in New York.

I loved sitting in the swing on her front porch almost every afternoon and evening in the spring and fall. She sat in her favorite rocker on the front porch and waited for us to come over and sit with her a while.

In 1960, television was quite innocent and subdued in what was shown on the screen. We all became involved with soap operas. It was great fun each day, guessing what would happen next. We liked joining in on all the gossip and couldn't wait to see what drama was in store for us on *All My Children* with Erica.

"Linda, Wanda!" We'd hear her sweet voice call each Sunday evening. "Why don't you girls come over and sit with me for a while?"

We'd race across the yard to see who got there first to enjoy the warm cookies awaiting us.

Mama Pearl had scrumptious strawberries growing in her backyard, beside her back doorsteps. They seemed to taste especially sweet when we picked them fresh from the strawberry patch.

Wanda and I spent hours in the hot sun with Mama Pearl as she planted each seed in her beautiful garden. With her wrinkled yet soft hands, she worked diligently, teaching us how to dig the hole just right before putting in the seeds and covering them with the black, silky dirt. Her cotton dress blew with the breeze as she knelt, weeding her garden with such patience.

I sometimes wondered as we worked if it was worth all that trouble. But, before we knew it, the fruit of her labor was realized as we walked down the rows of beans and peas. She always out picked us and brought in bowls of vegetables. Sitting next to us on her porch swing, she showed us exactly how to pinch off the ends of the beans so as to have no waste. We each had two bowls—one for the ends and one for the perfectly snapped beans, ready for cleaning and cooking.

Mama always smiled and looked forward to looking out her kitchen window as we ran home with fresh beans and peas for dinner. My favorite thing was Mama Pearl's juicy, sweet tomatoes. She showed me how to make the best tomato sandwich with mayo and salt and peeled tomatoes.

One night, Idgie and I spent the night with Mama Pearl, and the weather was frigid outside. The bathroom was off the back of the house, near the screened-in porch, which had been added on to her old house. There was no heat in the bathroom, so if we had to use the bathroom during the night, Mama Pearl brought out a big round pot for us to use. I was mortified at the thought of using a pot, so I made sure I went to the bathroom one last time before bedtime because I was determined I was not going to sit on that pot!

I loved watching Mama Pearl sweep her yard. She did not use a conventional rake, but instead used a broom made from long sticks tied together. It made a flowing kind of sweeping motion. We were all fascinated at how beautiful her yard looked after she finished sweeping. She worked diligently in her yard until she was in her nineties.

The old house was eventually torn down several years after hurricane Hugo came through our community. Mama Pearl went to be with her Lord in January 1994.

Years later, when I came home one day to visit, a deep sense of loss weighed heavily on my heart as I saw that vacant lot where her home once stood. The memories of her are forever imprinted on my mind. If I could speak to her today, I would say, "Thank you, Mama Pearl, for all the wonderful memories you gave us." She's one of those people I'm certain had a special crown to lay at Jesus' feet for all the kindness in her heart that she shared so willingly with us.

Mama Pearl taught me the meaning of empathy. She had that unique ability to understand the needs of others without expecting any personal attention. Many times, I saw her baking pies or making a basket of biscuits.

"Who are those biscuits for?" I'd ask.

"You know Mrs. Howell at church, don't you? She's been very sad lately since her husband passed away, so I am taking these biscuits to her today to cheer her up."

I realized through her example that it's important to look beyond myself and think of other people's needs.

Mama Pearl

BFF Idgie

Clean Little Feet

I don't want my girls running out with dirty feet.
What would the neighbors think?

Summer, 1965
Lydia, South Carolina
Linda

"Linda, Wanda! Come inside, girls. It's almost dark. Time to get cleaned up for bed." Mama called from the porch.

"But Mama, we already had our bath," I whined.

"Yes, but you went back outside to play afterward. What if something happens during the night and we have to rush out of the house, like to the hospital or something? I don't want my girls running out with dirty feet. What would the neighbors think?"

She winked at Wanda and me, and we both giggled.

The sweet, clean scent of Ivory soap takes me back to thoughts of Mama, those warm summer evenings. At ages six and four, Wanda and I seldom wore shoes. Living out in the country, we loved to run in our bare feet all day long. Mama was insistent that we went to bed with clean feet at bedtime.

I stood on the commode lid in our small half bath next to our bedroom. I put one foot at a time into the warm, sudsy water Mama had prepared in the sink. I watched her hands as she gently turned the Ivory soap over in the washcloth until it had enough soap to suit her. She took my foot in her hand and washed all the way up to my knee to be sure all the dirt was gone. Next, Mama lifted Wanda onto the commode lid and giggled with her as she washed her little feet.

By this time, our eyes were getting heavy. She helped us into our pretty pajamas, and softly tucked us into bed with a prayer and a kiss. Mama knelt by our beds beside us as we folded our hands in prayer and recited together:

Now I lay me down to sleep

I pray Thee, Lord, my soul to keep

Angels watch me through the night

And wake me in the morning light

If I should die before I wake

I pray, Thee, Lord my soul to take.

My Mama's servant heart reflected Christ to my sister and me. Her washing our feet has always reminded me of Jesus washing the disciples' feet. That one simple act, etched into my memory, has moved me to want to love and serve others well, expecting nothing in return.

Our Mama didn't have to wash our feet. I'm sure she was tired at the end of her day. We could have gone to bed with dirty feet. But that was not what this mother wanted for her newly adopted little girls. We were a gift from God to her. She treasured her time with us, even bedtime. We didn't realize it then, but she was teaching us how to love God, to make prayer time an important part of our lives, and to know that we could trust Him for our future.

My little sister and I crawled into bed, our fingers intertwined for security, and had sweet dreams because of her caring spirit and act of love to us. The memory of a mother's sacrificial love will be etched in my mind as long as I live, and that legacy will be passed on to my granddaughters.

#

Decades later, something on the front page of *The State* newspaper caught my eye. I very seldom sit still long enough to read the newspaper, but the "Mother's Day Writing Contest" caught my eye, along with, "Enter your poem or story about your mother and win the grand prize trip to Disney World!"

"That sounds like a perfect idea," I told my husband, Richard. "We've been talking about taking our daughters on a family vacation to Disney World. What if we won?"

"There's probably a slim chance, but you have a great poem. Why not go for it?" My sweet husband encouraged me.

But as I read the article, I realized that day was the deadline.

"I sure hope I can make it downtown in time," I said, dashing out the door, poem in hand.

It was almost 4:55 p.m. when I reached the newspaper's door.

"We are about to close, so run upstairs and hand in your entry," the lady at the front desk said as I ran up the stairs.

Out of breath, I handed the poem to the first person I saw.

"Here is a poem I wrote to my mother for Mother's Day a few years ago. I'd like to enter it in the contest. Am I too late?"

"No, ma'am, you just made it!"

I received a phone call at work a few weeks later on a Friday afternoon, and a lady told me I won the contest. She also said she just had to let me know that they all cried when she read the poem out loud to the other employees. My hand flew up to my mouth in disbelief.

I imagine Mama felt some excitement when she opened the mail to find a postcard telling her not to miss the Sunday morning paper. She said she could hardly wait for daybreak Sunday morning to run and get her newspaper. I had not told her I'd entered the poem.

Much to her surprise, she read my poem in the paper that day. I'd written it for her on Mother's Day in 1990.

The grand prize included a trip for two to any of four places: New Orleans, Gatlinburg, Orlando, or Nashville. Mama said she couldn't go anywhere because of Daddy's health, but she insisted Richard and I take our two daughters to Disney World in Orlando, Florida.

Richard and I did just that on Labor Day, September 5, 1994. We were so proud that the poem meant so much to everyone who read it.

My Special Mom

God chose you to be my mom
Before we ever knew,
His Sovereign Hand was planning
To give me a mom like you.
Though of your flesh, dear Mom,
I was not conceived,
Even so, you cared and filled
A very empty need.
Within my heart there is a place,
None else on earth can fill,
For you beside my bed sat
Whenever I was ill.
You gave me many happy times,
And fond memories to cherish.
My grateful heart wants you to know,
I'll never let them perish.
Reflecting on what might have been
Gives cause for me to shudder,
But God saw fit to intervene,
Thus making me your daughter.

Linda H. Summerford.

For many years, Mama taught Sunday school at Mt. Elon Baptist Church. One of her favorite students was Mike Bell. He was a few years older than I was, and, unbeknownst to him, my first crush. Mike wrote me a note recently about his memories of Mama and Daddy and our beautiful church in the country.

I have very fond memories of growing up in my church family of Mt. Elon. When I reminisce of those wonderful days, I recall many faces. People you could always count on to be there to offer kind words, support, and encouragement. Frances and Carwell Haney were two of those faces, accompanied by two little girls who would steal your heart and attention during a worship service. As planned, the worship service would be followed by my chasing Linda and Wanda around the magnolia and oak trees.

I know that Mrs. Haney loved me, because I had her so many times as a Sunday school teacher. Every time I was to move up to another department, she came with me. My wife says it might be that she was the only person willing to teach me. That suited me just fine because she always brought great food and snacks along and didn't tell my parents how badly I behaved. Being Baptist, as one might expect, no gathering was official unless food was served. One could always count on Mrs. Haney having some great dishes on the table. Following the meal, it was time to chase the Haney girls some more.

No summer was complete without vacation Bible school, and Mrs. Haney could always be counted on to try and teach us young hooligans a few verses from the Good Book. Following snacks, it was time for crafts. I still have the shoeshine box I built one year. Great days and wonderful memories.

#

I recall all the wonderful friends I made at Mt. Elon. Many of my close friends at West Hartsville Elementary School also attended church out in the country, at Wesley Chapel Methodist Church. Debbie Bass (Andrews) and I were inseparable. She recently shared some memories with me that I had actually forgotten. For instance, we had many of the same teachers. I loved Mrs. Gardner, who taught me to write cursive and draw butterflies. We both loved our music teacher, Mrs. Will, who taught us to play the autoharp in the fourth grade. Mama volunteered every year as a classroom helper. She always made the best cupcakes for all the children. Swinging high on the swings and climbing on the jungle gym were our favorite things on the playground. All the children loved the Easter egg hunts in the pine trees.

Debbie reminded me of the day we painted a mural on the hallway bulletin board when we found out President Kennedy had been shot. Debbie would spend hours at my house in Lydia. We would play dress up with our friend, Idgie. We thought we were too old to play with Wanda, and Mama often had to remind us to include her.

One of my dearest friends, Carolyn Kelly, told me that her fondest memory of my mom was when mom would bring her clothes that she had made just for Carolyn. Mom had done that in secret. I never even knew. Mom believed in doing things for others without recognition.

#

Mama insisted that I learn to hang clothes out on the line and fold them before bringing them in. Hanging the clothes was like a science. They had to be hung perfectly so that they could be folded without being ironed when they came down. The shirts were to be hung upside down at the seams. The slacks were to be unzipped and hung at the waist so the sun would hit them just right and they would not wrinkle.

Even as a ten-year-old girl, I remember putting the clothes basket in the red wagon because I was too short to reach the clothesline. I had to stand in the wagon to hang out all the clothes on the line, pulling it along as I connected each shirt with a clothespin. I was embarrassed that I had to hang Mama and Daddy's underwear on the line for the neighbors to see, so I always put them on the back line so they wouldn't be seen from the road. I spent many nights ironing my daddy's underwear, shorts, and T-shirts. I had to iron and fold the sheets just like Mama had shown me. For some reason, I enjoyed it all while listening to the Top 40 hits on the radio. I was so proud to bring Mama a basket full of folded and ironed clothes.

"Here's your five-dollar allowance," she would say, a big grin on her face.

I didn't wise up until years later that it was just busywork she gave me to keep me home and out of trouble.

Mama was such a beautiful seamstress. She always made her girls matching dresses. When we were little, Wanda and I were so proud of our matching red and white dresses Mama made for Christmas. They had bib-like tops with trim all around, called rickrack, from the shoulders to the waist and beautiful white buttons down the front.

One year, Mama gave us the book, *The Night Before Christmas*. We loved to sit cross-legged on the bed, listening to the words roll off her tongue into our minds. Before long, I had all the words memorized and I could turn the pages as I read the story to Wanda.

Around the time of my birthday, April 30, came another very exciting time for us—Easter. In Sunday school, we learned it's a time of celebration for the resurrection of our Savior. In school, we celebrated Easter with the Easter bunny and baskets full of candy.

What a great surprise it was for us as we woke up to the ringing of the doorbell on our first Easter morning. Wanda and I thought we had company visiting.

"Linda and Wanda," Mama said, "go answer the doorbell."

We looked at each other, puzzled. It was not often that we were told to answer the door.

We both ran to see who was there, but there was no one standing on the other side. Then we looked down—to see two baskets on the front steps. They were beautifully wrapped with colored cellophane wrapping paper and perfect bows on top, filled with jelly beans, candy eggs, marshmallow peeps, and a big chocolate bunny standing in the middle. We were only allowed to eat one piece of candy before church.

We were so excited to put on our new dresses that we forgot about the baskets, but only for a moment. Wanda and I walked into our room to see our beautiful dresses lying on our beds. Next to them, we saw tiny white purses and gloves. Easter hats were there, and on the floor were our new black patent leather shoes and white socks with lace all around. Mama even rolled our hair and added matching barrettes.

After we were both completely ready, we sat on the couch and smiled broadly for Mama to take pictures commemorating the special occasion. My dress was blue satin with lace along the bottom. Wanda's was similar but pink. We stood in front of the fireplace and took turns posing in chairs in the living room before we proudly hopped in the car to go to church.

After church, all the children in Sunday school headed outside for the annual Easter egg hunt. We were so excited to get back home to our baskets and candy. The candy lasted for several weeks because we could only have a few pieces a day.

I remember the first time we dyed Easter eggs with Mama.

"Linda, Wanda," we heard Mama calling. "Come to the kitchen. I have a surprise for you."

We ran as fast as our little legs would take us.

"What is it, Mama?" Wanda loved helping Mama in the kitchen.

"Slide your chairs up close to the counter. We're going to dye Easter eggs today so you can hide them at church."

She helped us bring two chairs from the kitchen table to the counter and turned them around for us to stand in. We each had a little wire with a circle at the bottom of it. Our eyes opened wide, and we squealed in delight when we dropped the tablet in the water, which turned different colors. Mama had already boiled about two dozen eggs and cooled them. She taught us to put the eggs on the wire and drop them into the colored water. We rolled the eggs around several times, watching in amazement as they changed color. Then we had to learn to lift them from the water to dry in the egg tray. Next, we put the eggs in our baskets and ran outside to hide them all afternoon.

Our legs were tired that evening, and we slept well with our baskets by our beds.

While April had brought my birthday, June 6 was time to celebrate Wanda's. Mama loved to hear Wanda's answer when people asked her, "When is your birthday, Wanda?"

"Chix-o-June," her sweet little voice answered.

All our friends came over for Wanda's party that year. Many cousins came with gifts in hand. We were all excited as she smiled with glee and blew out her four candles on the cake Mama had made for her. What a difference a year had made.

The doctor was right when he told Mama and Daddy that all Wanda needed was love.

Wanda and I loved the summertime at our new home in the country. We were not ever far away from Bubba. He followed our every move. He was in almost every picture Mama and Daddy took of us when we are in the yard playing. Whether we were riding our bikes, playing in the garden, or digging in the sandbox, you could find Bubba guarding his new responsibilities.

How fast our first year went by in our new home. Soon it was Christmastime again. In our matching pj's, Wanda and I ran into the den to see all our wonderful gifts. Daddy laughed as we opened each gift and held it up for the camera.

"Look, Mommy! Look, Daddy, at what I got from Santa!"

We were so happy we had been good all year, so Santa had come to our house. We loved our new dolls with matching strollers. I was especially proud of the bride doll I received, which I had seen in the store window.

I even got a drum set, and Wanda got a piano with a little stool to sit on. We sat on daddy's lap, handing him his Christmas gifts from Mama and us.

"Put your hats and sweaters on, girls, and come outside," we heard Daddy call.

We could hardly wait to see what else was in store for us. Outside, we found new, shiny bikes and batons to twirl. I was so excited to learn how to play my records on my new, pink record player. Wanda brought her doll over to dance to the music.

The sad years of our childhood faded into happy memories.

A Farmer's Hands

He came inside the house with tears in his eyes and said, "I'll never do that again"

Summer, 1966

Lydia, South Carolina

Linda

"Suey, suey, suey!" Daddy yelled, and all the pigs came running.

"Hurry, Wanda. Daddy is feeding the baby pigs."

I grabbed Wanda's hand as we ran barefoot up the hill. We didn't even care about the mud squishing between our toes. Laughing until we cried, we could barely make it to the pen.

"Suey, suey!" I copied Daddy. He looked at us and smiled.

"See, girls, here's some slops. Give some to the mamma pig. It's her favorite. He amazed me as I saw him stand among them, unafraid. They ate feverishly as if they might starve.

"Daddy, look, she's eating right out of my hand." My mouth dropped open in surprise.

Turning around, I saw Wanda rolling around in the mud, laughing.

"Wanda, get up. You're ruining your clothes." Daddy looked at us and realized he would be in big trouble with Mama when we got back home.

"Come on, girls, let's get you cleaned up before Mama sees you." He picked us up and stood us on the hood of his big car.

"All right, girls, stand still and turn around while I hose you off."

"That's cold, Daddy!" We squealed and giggled as we danced on his car.

When we arrived back home, Mama stood in the doorway, laughing.

"What in tarnation happened to you girls?" Mama winked at daddy because she knew this was the way he showed love to his little girls.

"Linda fed the pigs all by herself today," he said proudly. "What's for dinner?"

Daddy was a strong but loving man whose kindness helped Wanda and me overcome our fears. I do not recall ever being held in a man's arms where I felt safe before his. No one ever spoke the words "Daddy's girls" before he did.

I sometimes wished I'd been closer to Daddy when I was younger. I imagine most adults would probably say the same thing, but if we were not as close as we could have been, it was most likely more my fault than his. As a teenager, I'm sure I didn't realize what a gift he was to me. I never saw things through his eyes. Things would have been much different if I had taken the time to do that.

Daddy was not an affectionate man. In fact, at times, he could be rather distant. Looking back now, I wonder, was he unhappy, sad, or did he just feel inadequate raising two daughters? He was a quiet, kind man. I seldom heard him raise his voice, but with one look, he could discipline with his eyes.

Mama always said Daddy had a lot on his mind and was a deep thinker. He was always worried about providing for his family and keeping us safe.

One day I told Mama, "I don't ever remember Daddy spanking us. I remember you chasing us around the house with the flyswatter."

We both laughed.

"Well," she said, "he did spank you one time when you were little. He came inside the house with tears in his eyes and said, 'I'll never do that again.' He said it hurt him so badly when you looked at him with those crocodile tears streaming down your face that he swore he would never lay a hand on either of you again—and he never did."

One of Daddy's favorite things to do was to go to the Florence County Fair each fall.

"Wanda, Linda, go get your shoes on, it's time to go to the fair." Wearing his usual khakis and plaid shirt, he pulled the car around to the porch for us to load up. The musky smell of cherry pipe tobacco and spice penetrated the air as we climbed in the back seat.

"You look lovely this evening in your new dress, Frances." Daddy winked.

As we were getting out of the car, Daddy said, "What's our number one rule, girls?"

"Hold on to Mama or Daddy's hands." We replied in unison.

"What do you want to ride first?" He pointed to the boats.

"Yes, the boats." I grabbed Wanda's hand as we ran to get in line.

Daddy picked Wanda up as I climbed in the boat.

Ding, ding, ding, went the bell as we each pulled the chains. My first memory of my daddy laughing was when we were at the county fair.

The bright rainbow colors of the lights were mesmerizing—some blinking while others were on a strand flashing. My head was spinning as I tried to look up above the crowds. We had never seen so many lights, smiling faces, and laughter.

"Daddy, can I have cotton candy?" Wanda said with puppy eyes.

"Okay, but can you share with your sister?"

"Sure, Daddy. Finn, do you want cotton candy too?"

"Yes, but only on a stick." I grinned.

"A stick? Well, we will have to search for that. It's only in a bag here. Girls, stay with your mom and I'll go find cotton candy on a stick."

"Let's go ride Dumbo, Wanda. Mom, can we, please?"

"Okay, girls, but you know Wanda gets scared when she's up high, so Linda stay close to her."

"Wanda, look at Dumbo's ears, just like in the movie." I tried to keep her from being scared.

"Whee!" Wanda screamed, with her hair flying in the wind. The smells of elephant ears and hot dogs filled our noses. The ride came to a stop. Standing next to Mama was Daddy, with a big grin and cotton candy on a stick.

#

Wanda and I were six and four years old the first time we saw the ocean.

Hand in hand, we ran through the hot sand to the water. It was like the waves were calling me. The water swept over our feet and we jumped in.

"Wanda, look, the water is so high, it's up to my chest. Just then, a wave knocked Wanda down. She popped back up, screaming. I could hear daddy's feet splashing as he picked her up and said, "From now on, girls, you must hold my hand while you're in the ocean."

"Wanda, go play in the sand with Mama for a few minutes, and I'll come get you."

"Linda, grab my hands, I'll hold you up with each wave. When you see the wave coming, jump with me."

"Here it comes, Linda." He lifted me up. I could taste the salt water in my mouth and my eyes burned, but I screamed with excitement.

"Your turn, Wanda. It's so much fun!" We played in the sun and sand for what seemed like hours.

It was a special evening when we would all pack up and head down to the Myrtle Beach Pavilion to ride the many rides and eat our fill of hot dogs and ice cream. Daddy would give us tokens. I became an expert at skeet ball.

"Daddy, what's that big wheel over there. Can we ride it?"

"Sure, girls, here's two tokens. Hop on." The young man locked us in, but Daddy didn't trust it. He came over, lifted the bar up and down and then said, "Alright, now they can go."

We started going up. "Look, Wanda, the people are getting smaller and smaller. Let's wave at Mama and Daddy. But something wasn't right. I could feel Wanda start to panic.

"Sissy, are you okay?" She gave me that look, and I knew what was coming. With all her might, she let out the most horrible scream I had ever heard. She wouldn't stop screaming. Daddy heard her and ran over to the man controlling the ride.

"Stop this ride right now!" He shouted. "Bring my girls back down!"

The man started to argue with Daddy.

"Sir, I can't do that."

"Oh, yes you will. Or I'll do it myself." He reached for the huge lever.

The man saw the anger in daddy's face and was terrified.

The man reached over, pulled the lever and the ride began to move backwards. It came back down to a stop and Daddy was the first to greet us with Wanda still screaming. Daddy picked her up, grabbed my hand, and got us off that Ferris wheel.

"I'll never ride that again," I told him. And I have not to this day.

Mammy's Kitchen, Daddy's favorite breakfast restaurant, is still a favorite of ours today.

"Carwell, you know we will have to wait in line. I hope that's okay with you." Mama reminded Daddy.

"I'm so hungry, I don't care." He laughed.

I looked down the path to the front door and it seemed so far away. I could hear my tummy rumbling. But Mama was prepared with snacks.

"Here, girls, nibble on your strawberries. I know you're hungry too."

I learned patience from my daddy. He didn't mind waiting in line for an open seat in the restaurant.

"It's always worth it, to eat at Mammy's Kitchen," he assured us.

#

I love the song "Drive," by Alan Jackson. It reminds me of Daddy every time I hear it. The first time I heard the song on my car radio, I had to pull off the side of the road. I was crying uncontrollably. Immediately my mind wandered back in time, and I visualized him teaching me how to drive.

As soon as I turned sixteen, I'd begged to get my driver's license.

Daddy laughed. "Okay, but just realize that you may not pass the test the first time."

That made me even more determined to prove him wrong. I studied the driver's handbook from cover to cover. I even made up tests to prepare.

There was a grassy area of land next to the church. Handing the keys to me, Daddy would say as I ran to meet him, "Okay, let's go practice."

I was nervous but excited too. He set up two barrels at just the right distance and taught me how to parallel park.

When it came time to take the test, I could hardly sleep the night before. I passed with no problem. The officer even said he had never seen a teenager parallel park so perfectly. Daddy beamed with pride.

With my new permit in hand, it was time to drive on the highway. I felt so proud driving that brand-new '68 T-Bird, tan with the black top, through town with all my friends watching me. Daddy had paid cash for it.

I remember Daddy saying one time, "By the time you get to that speed limit sign ahead, you should have slowed down to forty-five."

I thought quietly for a moment, then asked, "So by the time I get to the next sign, I should be already going sixty?"

He did not like my sarcasm and just shook his head.

As we drove along the long, country road, buzzards flew over. I had always wondered why they did that, so I asked Daddy, "Why are those birds flying in circles like that?"

Being a man of few words, he just replied, "That's a sign of death."

My eyes got big as I looked at him.

"Not our death, silly," he said. "There's a dead animal on the road somewhere, and the buzzards are circling to tell the others where they can find a free meal."

"Oh, no, that's gross!"

Again, Daddy just shook his head.

Daddy was a proud man. We were not rich, but we thought we were. Family meant so much to him. We spent many Sundays sitting in the rocking chairs and porch swing at his sister Hannah's home, surrounded by cousins on the Haney side of the family. I can still taste the home-cooked meals topped off with her German Chocolate or Coconut Crème cakes. We'd stay until dark, filling our plates with second helpings of food, talking and playing for hours with aunts, uncles, and cousins.

The song by Holly Dunn also held a special place in my heart because it spoke of "Daddy's Hands." It was so well written and meaningful because the words described my memories of my Daddy's hands. His hands were big, rough, and calloused, but they always showed love.

My Special Daddy

You were a family man
So dependable and true
Always there for Mama and us
How we counted much on you.

When I was growing up
I was too busy to see
How reliable and special
A daddy could be.

But now that I am older
I have come to see
The numerous sacrifices
That you made for me.

There were beach vacations
And mountain trips too,
Travels to see family
All provided for by you.

In countless other ways
I was not deprived,
For it was you, Daddy
Who taught me how to drive.

In His providential love
God wanted a family unique,
And it took you, daddy,
To make it complete!

Linda H. Summerford

Two Weeks Too Soon

Richard obviously had no hesitation talking to old people.

Fall, 1968
Linda

"**Y**ou've got to meet this guy, Linda," my best friend Judy said as I slid onto the smooth, white leather seats of her candy-apple red Camaro. We were headed to school in her new car that her dad had given her as an early graduation gift.

"What's so special about this guy?"

"He's a senior, plays in the band—and he's very cute."

"I know, my friend at church told me I should meet him because he's interested in me. But I'm only fifteen, Judy, and I can't date until I'm sixteen, which is still two weeks away."

"Well, that's okay. You can still meet him and see if you like him."

"I suppose so. What do you know about him?"

"His name is Richard Summerford. He saw you in the hall at school the other day and told me he thinks you're pretty and that you have a beautiful smile. He wants to meet you. You're friends with Nancy, right?"

"How could he like my smile? My teeth are covered in braces. Yes, Nancy and I work together at Roses Dime Store. We're very close friends."

"Great! Her boyfriend is a close friend of Richard's. They're in the band together. You guys could even double-date in a few weeks."

I found out that Richard had been in the Hartsville Junior High and Hartsville High band for many years. He was the first chair and played the tuba or the sousaphone.

"Well, I'll have to wait and ask my parents. How old is he?"

"He's nineteen. He's been dating a girl awhile, but they recently broke up."

I frowned. "Okay, but he's kind of old for me. I don't know what Mama and Daddy will say about that."

"You can tell them he's a fine Christian guy. I know that for sure. He's active in the youth group at First Baptist."

"Sounds good to me, but I know what the sixteen- and seventeen-year-old so-called Christian boys are doing with the other girls in my church, and I want no part of that. I want a man who is truly living the Christian life and will respect me."

"I'll be sure to tell him your expectations." Judy smiled. "You don't have a thing to worry about."

Excited at my wonderful day, I ran in to tell Mama and Daddy what Judy had told me. I was talking so fast I ran out of breath.

"His name is Richard Summerford. He's a senior and a first-chair sousaphone player in the band." I smiled as I rattled off my exciting news.

Daddy's face darkened. "You are only fifteen years old, young lady, and you've never even dated. You are *not* dating a twenty-year-old man. They have only one thing on their mind at that age. You can't date until you're sixteen, and that's the end of it."

Daddy stomped out of the room.

Tears flowed down my face as I ran to Mama.

"Well, he's right, Linda." Mama sighed. "You can't date for two more weeks anyway. I'm not sure you're ready to date someone that old. How about starting with one of the boys your own age, maybe someone from church?"

"Mama, I've seen how the boys play around with the other girls in my class. They laugh and make fun of what they did with them. Then all the girls cry because they feel used by the boys. I don't want any part of that. They don't respect the other girls, and I couldn't live with myself and face them in church if they tried to do things to me."

I stood and squared my shoulders. "I've decided I'm waiting and saving myself for marriage. I'd rather date someone older who's serious about being only with me and wants to wait until marriage too. Everyone tells me that's how Richard is. So, in two weeks, I will go on a date with Richard. After you meet him, I know you'll feel the same way."

I wiped my face as I turned toward my room.

Mama's voice softened, and she came to me and hugged my neck. "There's no need to get so upset now. We'll find out more about Richard and his family. Maybe Daddy will feel better about him then. It's time for bed, so go get ready for tomorrow and we will talk more then."

Summers in South Carolina were always very hot. We had a huge attic fan in the hallway between the bedrooms. After the sun went down, Mama turned on the attic fan to draw the heat out of the house, and a cool breeze flowed through all our bedroom windows.

My room felt hot at the head of my bed, so I moved my pillows to the foot of the bed beside my windows. With the cool breeze on my face, I looked up at the full moon.

"Hello, God. It's me, Linda," I whispered. "Thank you for taking care of my family and me today. Thank you for my good report card and for the money Mama gave me for doing all my chores. I am happy she is so proud of me. Thank you for my sister, Wanda, and for all my blessings."

I paused, then blurted, "God, could Richard be the man you want me to marry?"

I looked up at God's face. I imagined He was looking at me through the full moon.

"I sure hope so," I continued, snuggling deep into my pillows. "I don't want to be hurt and made fun of like the other girls. Please give me peace of mind and assurance that you have sent him for me. Good-night, God."

Two weeks later, I was finally "sweet sixteen." It felt like the longest two weeks of my life. I felt so lucky and blessed to have a wonderful family. For my birthday, Mama and Daddy told me I could go to Bass Furniture store and pick out an entire bedroom suite. I'd selected the Spanish style. It was so much fun to put all my clothes neatly in the drawers—no more crowded dresser. I was so excited to finally be sixteen.

I opened my closet door to pick out one of my new outfits Mama had bought for my birthday—and I screamed.

"Mama! Come quick!"

"What in the world is wrong, Linda?" Mama raced down the hall, breathless.

"A rat! There's a rat on top of my clothes! How can I wear them with a rat crawling on them?"

Tears ran down my face.

Mama giggled. "Oh, my goodness, Linda. It's only a tiny little mouse. He must have come down from the attic."

"I don't care where he came from—just get him off my clothes!"

Mama took a breath. "Carwell! Come get this mouse out of Linda's closet."

Obviously, she was as scared of him as I was. They handed me my clothes, and I inspected them for rat droppings. Then I ran to my dresser to get my other clothes out of the top drawer.

And I screamed again.

"Now what?" Mama ran into my room again. "Another mouse?"

"No! The top drawer fell out and landed on my toe—it's bleeding! What else is going to go wrong on my sixteenth birthday?"

Holding my foot and bloody toe, I sat on my bed and cried.

"It looks pretty bad," Mama calmly said. "You'll probably lose that toenail."

"What? Lose my toenail? What a terrible birthday I'm having!" I complained through my tears.

Mama wrapped my toe tightly with bandages and sent me off to the bus stop with a big hug. "I'm sure things will only get better from here. Try to enjoy the rest of your day, sweetheart."

I shouldn't have worried, for it turned out to be a good day after all. The boys on the bus helped me walk and carried my books. I finally talked to Richard, since I could now date. He showed me lots of sympathy, and we planned our first date for Friday. Daddy said I had to double-date until he got to know who "this Richard boy" was. I didn't really mind—I felt safer with another couple too.

Finally, Friday arrived. I spent all afternoon primping with huge tin-can curlers in my hair. I selected just the right outfit and put on my makeup. Mama had made me a burgundy floral skirt and a top to match. The material was shiny, like satin, and the skirt flowed as I walked. Wanda sat on my bed and watched me, giggling.

I was nervous but excited as well.

Right on time, Richard showed up in his new Pontiac GTO. It was loud, and Daddy left the room when Richard came up the driveway. He was already mad, and he hadn't even met Richard.

Mama could see I was tearing up, so she went to get Daddy. He came back into the living room so he could "meet this old man coming to pick up my daughter."

I wanted so desperately for them to like Richard and give him a chance. This would be my first date, and I wanted everything to go perfectly.

"He will have to come in and speak to us, or you won't go." Daddy gave me a stern look.

Richard turned the car around in the driveway and parked. Then he came to the door and rang the doorbell.

I was not allowed to answer the door until the doorbell rang, so as not to seem too eager.

"Hi." I smiled as Richard came in the door. "Come on in. My parents want to meet you."

"Sure, I'd like to meet them, too," Richard said with a huge grin on his face.

We went through the introductions, and Mama pointed to the couch for Richard to sit.

"Thank you," he politely responded.

"So, tell me about yourself, Richard," Daddy quickly questioned.

Richard obviously had no hesitation in talking to "old people." We spent what seemed like an hour talking about Richard's job at A&P and his many years in the marching band at Hartsville High School. I could tell my daddy liked him already, even though he would never admit it to me.

Shoney's was the big hangout for all the teenagers. If you're really on a date, you didn't stay in Hartsville, I learned. You went to Florence to ride around to see and be seen. That night, we doubled-dated with our friends, Ricky and Nancy. Around and around we drove through Shoney's parking lot, sitting close and waving to all our friends. I was beaming with pride.

We dated for almost two years. The first year was difficult. Daddy still didn't trust Richard because of his age. Richard tried very hard to win his trust. He would always arrive fifteen minutes early and have me back home at least fifteen minutes before my curfew. The porch light would come on quickly as we walked up. I'm sure that was to discourage any goodnight kissing. We learned to work around that problem by kissing goodnight in the car.

There were arguments about including my little sister on all our dates, and the threat of a shotgun during those two years, but finally, my parents got to know Richard and loved him too.

The day before Valentine's Day, 1971, Richard picked me up for our date. When we arrived at our favorite "parking" spot, at Lake Robinson, he asked me to open the glove box and get something out for him. When it fell open, there was a beautiful black box with a red ribbon tied on it.

My eyes filled with tears instantly as I turned my head toward him crying. He told me later he had driven all the way to Rock Hill, South Carolina, to get the ring. He couldn't decide which size to get me, so he drove back and forth three times that day, each time exchanging the ring for a bigger diamond. He settled on the half-carat solitaire diamond. It looked huge to me. I quickly screamed yes through my tears.

We planned the wedding for August thirteenth the following year. He said he felt that the number thirteen was our lucky number since we got engaged on the thirteenth, so we decided to get married on the thirteenth.

Our wedding was beautiful, and the church was filled to capacity with all our friends and family. Richard was my first date and my last. We have now celebrated our fiftieth wedding anniversary. God has blessed us with two beautiful daughters, Jeni and Lisa, and five grandchildren—Aydin, Averi, Rilyn, Leland and Emerson.

The Letter

Girls, how would you like to meet your sister?

October 1973
Linda

I smelled fried chicken as I walked in the door. Mama had been up all morning cooking my favorite meal. She always rose before the sun to cook on Sundays because she never missed church.

Sundays were always special at our home, and Mama was a great cook. Even after getting married and moving away, I enjoyed making the long trip home for a much-anticipated home-cooked meal.

But this Sunday was like no other.

Richard was sick, so he didn't make the trip with me from Columbia to Hartsville. After we got our fill of Mama's wonderful meal, we all moved to the den. Daddy sat in his favorite chair and Mama in hers. Wanda and I relaxed on the couch, beginning our conversations with small talk about events in our lives since last I was home. I was twenty-one years old and had been married for two years. Wanda was nineteen. She had graduated high school and was still living at home.

All of a sudden, Mama looked at Daddy. He stared back.

Something's up.

They moved their gaze toward Wanda and me, and Mama took a deep breath.

"Girls, your daddy and I have something important to discuss with you."

Wanda and I turned our heads toward each other with puzzled looks in our eyes.

I immediately began to panic, my heart pounding as if it might jump out of my chest.

Wanda's expression matched mine. Is one of them sick? Does one of them have cancer? What could be the important news they were so serious about?

Mama got up from her chair and walked into the bedroom. No one said anything for a moment.

When she returned, she sat down with a letter in her hand.

Wanda and I glanced at each other.

Then Mama asked a question that shocked us to our core.

"Girls, how would you like to meet your sister?"

She had a big smile on her face.

"What?" we said in unison. "We have a sister?"

Until that day, Wanda and I had never been told we had an older sister. Of course, we both burst into tears. We looked at Daddy, and even he was getting choked up.

"I was at my desk at work the other day when my phone rang. The lady on the phone asked, 'Is this Frances Haney?' 'Yes,' I replied, 'this is she.' Then she asked about my plans for lunch that day. I thought it was an odd question for her to ask, but I stuttered, 'I have no plans.

Why do you ask?' She then said, 'You need to come to the Department of Social Services office. I have some very important news for you.'"

Wanda and I held hands as Mama continued.

"I couldn't imagine what in the world she would need to see me about, but, of course, I went straight there on my lunch hour. When I arrived, the social worker handed me this letter. I read the letter and looked at the photograph enclosed. The letter is signed, 'Martha.' She says in her letter that she wants to meet her sisters at least once before she dies."

Mama stood then and passed the letter over. "Here is the letter and the photograph of your sister."

Wanda and I sat close to each other, and I read the letter out loud while we both wiped tears from our cheeks.

Dear Mr. and Mrs. Haney,

My name is Martha Kennemore. I have been searching for my sisters, Linda and Wanda, for many years. I was given your names by a dear social services caseworker, Mrs. Calhoun. She has given me permission to write you with my desire to meet my sisters.

As a little background on me, I graduated high school and attended college for two years. I have been married for several years. My husband, Mickey, and I live in Greer, SC. I am employed with Allen Bennett Hospital in Greer and Mickey works for GE in Greer.

At the age of four, I remembered that I had two younger sisters, but we have been separated. I did not understand what had happened at that time. I grew up in foster care all my life. At the age of sixteen, I began my search for my sisters. I was told at that time that my sisters had been adopted at a young age, and that I could not see them until Wanda was eighteen. I waited a few more years to continue my research. By that time, I was twenty-two years old, Linda would have been twenty-one, and Wanda was nineteen.

Let me express my feelings about my sisters. You cannot imagine the pain in my heart as I think about my little sisters and all the love I have for them. Just to know that there are two little girls out there who are my blood sisters, and I cannot put my arms around them to hug them and tell them how much I love them, brings tears to my eyes and an ache in my heart.

Mrs. Haney, I do not want to hurt my sisters in any way. I just want to see them at least once before I die. If you can agree to this, it would make me very happy. Thank you for all you've done to take care of my sisters all these years. I look forward to meeting you so that I can thank you personally.

Love, Martha.

We looked at the photo again and again—she looked like Wanda and me, combined. She had brown eyes like Wanda, but her face and smile looked like me. We looked closely at her handwriting.

"It's just like mine. How eerie is that?" I said.

"When can we meet her?" Wanda asked.

"Well, you can imagine how shocked your father and I were when we saw this letter." Mama's lips tightened. "You need to know that when we adopted you, we were told that there were more siblings in the family, but they never told us whether they were boys or girls, or how many others there were. We were only told the other children were not released for adoption. I do remember when we first brought you home that, you, Linda, kept asking for Martha. I did not know if that was a friend or someone you were missing from the foster home, until I read this letter signed 'Martha.' If we had known that you had another sister who needed adopting, we would have taken her too."

She looked at Daddy, and he nodded.

"We were somewhat skeptical about who this person is, so we did do some background research on Martha, and were thankful to find out that even though she was never adopted, she turned out to be a lovely lady," Mama added.

"The man in the photograph is her husband, Mickey," Daddy said, his voice gruff.

Mama took a breath, "Your dad and I have discussed this letter a lot this past week. We want you to know we understand if you want to go be a part of that family now. We feel we have done our job. We have given you a good home, and now you both are over eighteen and can make your own decision about staying with us."

Wanda and I looked at them with shock on our faces.

"What do you mean, we can go 'be with that family'?" My eyes pricked with unshed tears. "We will never leave you. This is our home. We want to meet Martha and get to know her, but you are our parents. That will never change."

"Well, we are glad to hear that, but this all may change if you meet her. But your father and I felt we could not keep this from you. We wouldn't want you to find out later we had received this letter and not told you about it." Mama dabbed at her eyes. "So, whatever the consequences, we had to share this with you."

"We do want to meet Martha, Mom, but this is our home," I said. "And you are our mom and dad. Nothing will ever change that."

"Yes, that's how I feel, too." Wanda nodded.

"Okay. I'll call the social worker back tomorrow and see what we need to do next, so you can meet your sister."

It was a long drive back to Columbia that day. After talking all afternoon about this wonderful news, I cried all the way home.

I have another sister. Why didn't she stay with us and get adopted, too? What kind of childhood did she have? How I wish so much she could have grown up with Wanda and me.

Thoughts kept racing through my mind. But I knew there must have been a reason, and it was something that could not be changed.

Still, I couldn't wait to meet her.

Later that week, Mama called.

"All the arrangements are being made. We have to wait now on social services to finalize the plans. I'll let you know when and where we will meet Martha."

It seemed like months went by, though it only took a few weeks to finalize the arrangements. It was Thanksgiving week. We all met at Mama's for our annual Thanksgiving turkey and dressing dinner.

This Thanksgiving was different from all the ones before. The conversation around the table was all about meeting our big sister.

Finally, the big day arrived: November 23, 1973. I had spent the night at Mama's, and we all drove to Columbia together. Daddy drove while Wanda and I sat in the back seat. The ride was surprisingly quiet. We all couldn't stop thinking about how our lives would change after this day.

We walked quietly into the cold, white building—the Rutledge Building in Columbia, South Carolina—all the way up to the seventh floor. We were instructed to sit in a small room and wait while the social workers went to get Martha, who was waiting in another room.

The room was cold, and it had no windows. I fiddled with the hem of my skirt, and Wanda's hands were shaking.

"What does she look like now?" Wanda would ask every few minutes. "Will she like us?"

Suddenly, the door opened. A social worker in a blue suit and fluffy white shirt poked her head in.

"Girls, I'd like you to meet, Martha, your sister!"

And there she was.

Martha had cut her long hair. It was brown and cut short up to her ears. She wore a beige checked top with tan slacks. She burst into tears as she grabbed both Wanda and me. Martha was much taller than both of us. I thought she was so pretty, and her sweet smile was full of kindness. There wasn't a dry eye in the room. I could hear everyone sniffling, even the social worker.

We all hugged tightly for a long time, crying all the while. I looked over Martha's shoulder as she hugged me and saw my daddy, wiping his face with his handkerchief—I had never seen my daddy cry.

What a Thanksgiving it was that year. We talked for a long time with Martha and Mickey's mother, whose name was also Frances.

There were so many questions to answer, but many of those questions had no answers for us, at least not now.

"Well, girls, I have another surprise to share with you," Martha said with a big grin on her face.

We couldn't imagine what other surprise there could be.

"You also have a brother. His name is David. I have lost contact with him, but I think he may still live near the Greenville area. I'll work on locating him if you want to meet him, okay?"

"Sure, we want to meet him, Martha. We had no idea there were four of us." Wanda and I hugged each other tightly and cried.

I looked at Martha and said, "I used to look up at the moon before I went to sleep during my teen years, wishing I had an older brother to watch over me. Maybe in my heart, I knew he was out there." Martha grabbed me with another bear hug. She promised to try to locate David for us so we could meet him too.

After we all calmed down, we went outside and took lots of photographs to commemorate this special day. Hunger pangs began to stir our stomachs, so we all decided to go eat together at Shoney's restaurant in Columbia. We were the last ones to leave the restaurant before it closed for lunch. We stood in the parking lot hugging and taking more photographs before we had to let Martha go back to Greer, South Carolina, where she lived at that time.

Over the next months, we got together with Martha as much as we could. It was as if we had known each other all our lives. Small things surprised us at how much we were alike—even down to liking the same nail polish color. Martha wrote us many letters. We exchanged cards on each holiday, excited to pick out cards for "our sister."

"Have you noticed, Wanda," I said one day as we were shopping for Valentine's cards, "none of the Hallmark cards really fit our situation. There are no cards for a sister we didn't grow up with." Many times, we had to get blank cards and write in our sentiments for the occasion. Years later we noticed cards written for "a special sister" that were perfect for our new sister.

Martha & Mickey

Our First Meeting!

Reunion with a caseworker - 1981

The Guitar Man

I kept repeating your names in my mind so I wouldn't forget.

December 1990
Linda

I'd had a difficult, strenuous day at work, and the girls were fast asleep. I decided to run a long hot bath, when suddenly my phone rang.

Who could that be at this hour?

The soft voice of my sweet sister Martha was on the other end of the line.

We called each other often, even though it was long distance and cost a lot of money. We tried not to call too often because it seemed when we did, we had so much to share, and we were still on the line an hour later.

But this call was different.

Again, our lives were about to change.

Martha asked the usual questions about the family. Then she paused a moment.

"Linda, hon, how would you like to meet your brother?"

Silence. I couldn't speak, let alone breathe. *My...brother?*

Finally, I caught my breath. "What, my brother? Do you know where he is? Does he want to see us? Why now? Why has he not wanted to meet us before now?"

Questions flowed from my mind and heart.

Martha's voice was gentle. "David said he felt obligated to stay with our father because he was so sick, but since our father had refused to have anything to do with us, I assume because of his own guilty conscience, David waited until his death to contact us again. David said he was afraid that if we ever found him, we would naturally want to meet our biological father, and David knew we would be rejected instantly. He could not let that happen. He waited until our father died, even though it took fifteen years of waiting. David says that sometimes he wishes he had not waited but felt he had to protect us from the emotional trauma of rejection."

"We must respect him for that and love him all the more. We still have many years ahead of us to spend with our special brother and sister. We can begin to make our memories now," I said. But I still had questions running through my mind.

"I'll work out all the arrangements and call you back soon. Love you."

We began making those memories on November 19, 1990. All the plans had come together without a hitch.

That morning, Wanda came to my home in Columbia, and we anxiously got ready to go meet our brother. We talked constantly as we put on our makeup and fixed our hair. So many questions filled our minds. Would he like us? What does he look like? Does he favor me or Wanda? Is he sweet? Is he the kind, loving brother we have always dreamed of?

We were to soon find out.

Before we went to meet David, I told my friend from church, Eric Slagle, about meeting our brother for the first time. A photographer, Eric insisted on being there to document the special day for us.

We drove to the Embassy Suites hotel in Columbia, South Carolina that afternoon and parked. Nervously, we exited the car and began walking toward the hotel.

Martha and David didn't wait for us to get inside. They came running out of the hotel arm-in-arm to greet us. Eric was filming all the while.

Tears ran down Eric's face as he witnessed four children meeting after more than thirty years of separation. We stood huddled in a headlock for what seemed like an hour, looking at each other and crying.

David couldn't stop crying. He kept looking at us, stroking our hair and faces.

"I can't believe this day is here at last," David said over and over.

Finally, we stepped inside the hotel. The surroundings were beautiful, with waterfalls and plants everywhere. The camera was rolling, but we didn't even notice.

Martha had reserved a table in a private corner of the hotel restaurant where we could sit without being disturbed or without disturbing others with our crying and laughing. We had a sweet, young waitress. She was overcome with emotion, too, when we told her that today we four were meeting after all these years. She put her hand over her mouth and tears streamed down her face. She told the other waiters, and they offered us a bottle of champagne. David said he would take it home to put on his mantle as a memento of this wonderful day. That sweet waitress kept coming to our table, asking us if we needed anything, and then she took out a tissue to wipe her eyes. We took a picture of her so we could remember her sweet face.

None of us remember what we ate that day. I do recall we had a salad, and the lunch was a beautiful spread, a wonderful display of every kind of food imaginable. We sat for the longest time, sharing pictures and papers that we had on small portions of our childhood, the adoption, and the separation.

"I remember when I was about seven years old," David told us through tears. "You were still very young. I knew you were being adopted, but I was so afraid I would forget your names. When I went to bed at night, I would keep repeating your names in my mind— Linda Gail, Wanda Elaine—over and over as I fell asleep."

This is the first time Wanda and I learned what our original names were.

David added, "I thought that when I got older and I wanted to find you, I didn't want to forget your names."

I imagined a little boy with such a heavy burden on his heart. David had lived his entire life with the misplaced guilt of not being able to keep his sisters with him. He, too, was only a child who could do nothing to keep his family together, but he felt responsible for losing his sisters.

Today, we would be together, never to be separated again.

We decided to look for a photo shop that could develop our film while we waited, so each of us could have memories of this wonderful day to take with us. We drove to Dutch Square Mall, but the camera shop manager said they did not provide one-hour service on Sundays. We then decided to walk around the mall and spend more time together, still taking pictures at every stop. The mall was decorated beautifully for Christmas with lights and decorations everywhere.

Suddenly, we saw Santa in the middle of the mall. We looked at each other. We are all thinking the same thing: We had never been able to sit on Santa's lap together as children.

Giggling like kids, we stood in line with all the little children waiting to sit on Santa's lap and have our picture taken, just as if we were kids. We told Santa what a special day this was. He laughed and enjoyed being a part of this momentous occasion.

We were children of one family, together again.

Next, we drove to my home so David could meet Richard and Wanda's husband, along with all of David's new nieces and nephews. We spent the rest of the day taking hundreds more pictures.

David told us he could sing and play the guitar and that he was in a band. Richard brought out his guitar, and David sang a beautiful song for all his sisters. We were all overwhelmed as we sat on the couch next to him and listened to his sweet voice, which we wished we could have heard so many years ago. David said it felt so good to hear the children call him Uncle David. He was so touched that everyone accepted him instantly into his new family. It was as if he had always been there in our hearts, even though we never knew about him.

David told us how he'd enlisted in the navy but had been unable to serve for long. There are a series of tests each man must go through to see if he is "seaworthy," and those tests include mental evaluations. Each enlisted man must speak with a psychologist to determine whether he can survive months at sea in a submarine or on a naval ship. David explained how he told the psychiatrist about his early childhood. The psychologist asked to put him under hypnosis so David could reveal how bad the situation was.

After waking from the hypnotic state, David asked the doctor what he said while under hypnosis.

The doctor just shook his head. "I'll never tell you, but I'm afraid I must inform you that you cannot serve in the navy."

David was only enlisted for four months before he was honorably discharged.

We wanted to know what had happened to us on that fateful day.

On the first day we met David, as we sat together in my living room, he was still choking back tears and stroking our hair as he tried to remember the details.

David said he was only five years old when our world fell apart, but he remembered that day vividly.

"I had already seen unspeakable horrors no child should witness," he said quietly, running a shaky hand through his hair. "Many times, I hid behind the couch with all three of you, sheltering your ears from the yelling and cursing going on between our so-called parents. They didn't deserve to be parents. Our impoverished house was more like wild animals living together. I often wondered why these people were even living in the same house if they hated each other so much. Not a day went by that I didn't want to take all of you and run away. But where would we go? Who would help us?"

He described how we were always hungry, always cold, always crying.

"Wanda, you were only a few months old, and I was afraid you weren't going to live much longer. You were coughing and screaming all the time. When I picked you up, your body was hot from fever, yet cold because there was no heat in the house. I knew you were hungry, but what could I do to help you? I was so worried and scared."

David struggled to breathe and talk through the tears streaming down his face. We waited patiently for him to regain his composure.

"The day it all ended, I heard our mother slam the door as she cursed at our father and left. He told her she'd better not ever come back." His jaw tightened. "She didn't turn to hug us goodbye or even attempt to take us with her. She just left us there. Alone. To fend for ourselves.

"Suddenly, our father came running into the room. He ignored Wanda's screams from the bottom drawer of that old dresser and walked straight to me.

"'What's going on?' I asked him, but I got no response. I asked again and again.

"'Shut up!'" he yelled at the top of his lungs. I remember the hatred in his eyes—he reminded me of a rabid wolf. He walked toward me with a thick rope in his hands. I'd seen him use that same dirty rope in his work as a house painter. I kept wondering why he was bringing that rope toward me. I got up and tried to run away, but he caught the back of my shirt and threw me to the floor.

"'Sit down and shut up!' he continued to yell at me. I knew if I tried to run again, he would beat me senseless, so I surrendered."

David was quiet for a moment, remembering. Then he continued.

"He took the rope and pulled it through my legs, and then several times through the legs of a heavy old chair, until it was so tight, I started to cry from the pain."

"'Stop that crying or you'll get worse than this!' he screamed. So, I just lay down on the floor and hid my tears. I couldn't watch as he grabbed you, Martha." David looked at Martha, whose eyes were red with tears as she sat there on my living room sofa, her hands between her knees. "You were only about four years old. You'd been coughing a lot, and your face was red. I knew you must have had a fever. You were screaming, too, but he just ignored your cries and cut the rope long enough to wrap around your little legs as he secured the rope to another piece of furniture. You continued to scream and cry but finally cowered in fear."

Taking another deep breath, David continued. "I remember he cut the rope again and pulled you over to him next, Linda. You were only about two years old and didn't understand what was happening. None of us did. You started to try to squirm away, but he grabbed your legs and pulled you toward him. I could see the fear in your eyes, but you refused to cry. You were so afraid of him that you just went limp and closed your eyes. Again, he ran the rope around another leg of the heavy chair and pulled it tightly. I saw your tiny legs begin to bleed from the rope burns, and I turned my head away, afraid for him to see my tears."

David had to stop talking for a while again as we put our arms around him.

David turned his head and eyes as he took Wanda's face and cradled it in his hands.

"Wanda, you were only eight months old and very sick. You were rarely held unless I held you myself. I watched in horror as our father moved to the dresser drawer. I was afraid of what he was going to do to you.

"You began to scream from hunger and fear, but he never even flinched. His face had a blank look on it, as if he had no feeling.

"He just took the rope and tied your little legs to the dresser handle. I thought how foolish that was because you could not even sit up alone. But the man I saw standing over you was a man out of his mind with rage. I stayed still on the floor and pretended not to watch out of the corner of my eye as he turned to leave the house. I waited a few minutes to be sure he was gone."

David looked at each of us in turn.

"I—I couldn't do anything. Couldn't reach Wanda. She was crying for a long time, but finally, she stopped. I guess she just gave up and fell asleep. I was still shaking, both from fear and the cold. I struggled for a long time to untie my legs, but it was no use. The knots were too tight. Finally, I just gave up and laid my head on the cold, hard floor until I fell asleep.

"Suddenly, I heard footsteps. It sounded like someone was quietly walking on the front steps of the house. I couldn't move to see who it was. I thought it might be our father, so I put my head down and pretended to be asleep.

As I turned my head to see who it was, I saw a lady slowly pushing the door open. I'd seen her before. She was the lady who came to check on us sometimes. I wasn't really afraid of her, but I didn't know why she was there. I started to cry. I was hoping she was there to help us, but I knew, too, that every time she came, we were taken away to foster homes. Sometimes we were separated, and I didn't want that to happen again. I couldn't fight, so I sat still and watched and listened as she softly spoke to us and tried to remove the ropes.

"'Don't be afraid, children,' she'd softly said. 'I'm here to help you.' She kept repeating that over and over again. I don't remember her name, but I'll never forget her beautiful green eyes and soft voice.

"I know I was just a child, but for many years I wondered if she was real, or did I just dream God sent an angel to rescue us.

"The lady put us in the back seat of her car. We were very dirty and cold. I remember her laying her coat down for us to sit on and putting a blanket around all four of us huddled together. I'm sure we were a sight to see. But nothing seemed to rattle her. I still remember her kind voice constantly talking softly to us. We were taken somewhere and given baths and clean clothes. I kept trying to hold on to Martha's hand so they wouldn't take her from me, but I remember when they pulled her away, and I was so afraid I might never see any of you again.

"I was sent to stay with a family who already had a couple of kids older than me. Nights were especially hard for me. I kept repeating your names, Wanda Elaine, Linda Gail, and Martha Ellen.

"In my young mind that was all I knew to do—to try not to forget your names so that one day, I could find you again."

Music seemed to calm David's nerves so he picked up the guitar and played a few more songs for us. I found myself staring at him and my heart melting as I absorbed his story.

After sharing some drinks and snacks, we posed for pictures again and again. The children were so kind and had a fun day with their new uncle.

We made plans to get together again as soon as we could. For the next several years, the four of us sent cards on our birthdays and tried to talk on the phone weekly.

Over time, it became apparent that David was avoiding meeting with us. He told Martha that it was hard for him to see us, for every time he did, the memories of the past haunted him for many nights to follow. He would have nightmares of those horrible days. He began to become more reclusive over the years and eventually did not respond to our calls.

Martha, Wanda, and I stayed in touch and have done so until this day, but we lost contact with our brother.

The day we met - 1990

She'll be Right Back

*Mama saw him wink his eye when she called his name
as they wheeled him away.*

December, 1994

My special Daddy went to be with the Lord on Monday, December 5, 1994. He had been ill for quite some time.

In 1989, he'd suffered a ruptured intestine. It was on Thanksgiving Day. My phone rang as we were packing to come home for our annual Thanksgiving dinner.

"Linda," Mama said softly over the phone. "There will be no Thanksgiving dinner at home today. Meet me at the hospital. Your daddy is very sick. Please hurry."

The doctor later told us that if Daddy had not come to the hospital when he did, he would have died within hours.

Dr. Moyd left his mother's Thanksgiving table to rush to the hospital for Daddy. Thankfully, they were able to save his life. Daddy, however, began to decline in health from that point on.

He was able to survive a second operation six weeks later to reverse the colonoscopy, but he suffered several mini-strokes over the next few years. He had a blood clot in his leg, but they were able to keep it from traveling to his heart. He then suffered from congestive heart failure and was on medication for the fluid to keep it from destroying his heart.

The last problem Daddy had was pneumonia in October 1994. This took a lot out of him physically, for he had so much trouble breathing. It was a tremendous strain on his heart, also. Soon after Thanksgiving, Dr. Evans took Mama aside and told her things did not look well. He felt it would be miraculous if Daddy made it to Christmas.

On Sunday, December 4, Mama called to let me know I needed to come home to help her. We had planned to visit after lunch that day, but I immediately prepared my suitcase to stay for a few days.

Mama had been such a dedicated nurse to Daddy. She never wanted to leave the house. Since I had come to stay awhile, the next morning after I arrived, I insisted she go ahead and run a few errands. The date was Monday, December 5.

At approximately 10:30 a.m., Mama said she would run to the bank and maybe the grocery store. I felt I would be fine as long as she left me both the doctor's and neighbor's phone numbers. After Mama left, I went in to see if Daddy needed anything. He could hardly speak, for he was so weak. I lifted his head and gave him a sip of water.

I then tried to talk with him a little. I asked if he needed anything.

"No," he answered.

I asked if he wanted me to read to him.

"No," he said again.

He seemed to be asking where Mama was, so I told him Mama would be right back, that she'd just gone to the store.

".... Be right back."

"Yes," I said. "She'll be right back."

I asked him if he wanted to hear the radio. He just slowly shook his head and said, "No."

I thought he was trying to say something else to me, so I leaned in closer and asked, "Did you say something, Daddy?"

He just took one deep rattled breath and would not respond to me.

Of course, I began to panic. I jumped up on the bed and began to softly hit his cheeks, trying to get a response. I remember actually opening one of his eyes. There was no focus, just him staring straight ahead. He did not open them again.

"Daddy!" I called his name loudly several times.

He did not respond.

I began to pump his chest in a vain attempt at CPR. I realized I was still getting no response.

At this point, I decided I needed to call someone for help. I rushed into the kitchen to find the phone. I saw the number for Dr. Evans there on the counter. Dialing his number, I ran out of the house to the neighbor's house. I didn't want to wait to dial her number, so I ran to get her as I called the doctor.

I remember I could hardly speak to the doctor's office. I was shouting and crying to them that I needed someone to help me with my daddy and for them to get Dr. Evans on the phone.

I ran back into the house with the neighbor as I was still talking with the doctor's office. This all took place in about thirty to forty-five seconds. I continued my attempt at CPR.

Within about a minute, Dr. Evans called back. He said for me to let the EMS take care of Daddy. He tried to calm me down because I was shaking so hard and screaming into the phone.

Then I asked if I could go with Daddy to the hospital in the ambulance. He said I must stay at the house to wait and bring Mama to the hospital.

I called Daddy's name over and over. Then I realized I'd never called for the ambulance.

I quickly dialed 911 and began to shout that I needed someone to help me with my daddy. Later, I realized why two ambulances came to the house. The doctor had also called for the ambulance. They rushed in to work on Daddy. The EMS workers told me that they could see I was using CPR on him because his chest was red. I had done my best. They said they were getting a weak pulse. They kept asking us to leave the room and watch for visitors coming to the door.

Within minutes, Mama returned. She had decided not to go to the store but only the bank because she had seen the ambulance pass. As she drove up, I ran to her, crying that something had happened to Daddy because he would not talk to me.

She ran into the house and straight to his room. They were still trying to revive him.

She said she saw his eye wink at her when she called his name.

EMS put Daddy into the ambulance and sped away.

As all this was happening, my neighbors came running into the house. Our neighbor, Herbert King, had been driving up for a visit. Reba Best, our friend and neighbor, also came running when she saw the ambulance.

I was ready to go to the hospital when Reba put her arm around me and softly whispered in my ear, "Hon, you are barefoot. Go put on some shoes before you leave."

Mr. King drove us to the hospital. Shortly after we arrived, the nurses called us into a private room and said the doctor would meet with us soon.

I knew then that Daddy did not make it.

Dr. Evans came in and looked at Mama and shook his head. "I'm so sorry, Frances, but we could not revive him—he's gone."

Of course, we all cried, and Dr. Evans held Mama in his arms a long time.

Daddy's sister, Aunt Hannah, had met us at the hospital and was also in the room with us. She had just lost her brother. She was now the last child left in her immediate family. Mama had lost the man she had been married to for over forty-three years. Someone told me they thought Daddy had waited to die until he knew Mama had left the house so she would not have to be there when he passed away.

Wanda and I had now lost our "Special Daddy." My little girls had lost the only "Papa" they had ever known. Wanda's boys had lost their Papa Haney. It was a day of great loss, a day we will never forget or ever overcome. Time will heal, as they say, but the memories of this wonderful man are in our hearts forever.

When we got back home and I helped Mama clean his bedroom, I noticed the poem that I had written for Daddy was hanging on the wall beside his bed. I asked the church secretary if I could add it to the back of the program for his funeral.

My husband, Richard, spoke at his service these wonderful words about our "Special Daddy."

Carwell Haney
December 7, 1994

There were so many things that impressed me about this man, Carwell Haney. He was a man who loved his family. Mr. Haney dearly loved his wife, Frances, and was devoted to her. He showed this by doing special little things which expressed his love. There was one thing that stood out in my mind. When Frances went to work, Carwell would go out every morning, no matter the weather, to check her automobile to make sure everything was working properly before she would leave. He would pull the car up to the door and make sure it was warm for her. This impressed me so that even today, I do this same thing for my wife.

Carwell Haney loved his two brothers and his sister. Many times when we were visiting he would talk about them and show his concern when they were sick or hurting. He had a deep, special love for his sister, Hannah. Carwell loved his two daughters, Linda and Wanda, as well as his "other" daughter, Martha. I remember when I asked him for Linda's hand in marriage, he looked me in the eye and said, "You better take good care of my daughter." He even reminded me of that on many occasions. He was a good example for me.

Carwell was a man who cherished his grandchildren, Jennifer, Lisa, Phillip and Jon. Any time they were sick or upset, he would express his concern by suggesting that we as parents needed to do something to make things better for them. He didn't want his grandchildren to be hurting or wanting for anything. He always had such a wonderful smile on his face when he saw them.

Carwell was a man who loved good gospel preaching. Many times we would discuss sermons of men he admired; men such as Billy Graham, Jerry Falwell and David Ring—the pastor in Florida who has cerebral palsy, and of course his pastor here at Mt. Elon, Robin King.

Carwell Haney was a man of few words, but when he spoke, you better listen, because it was important. His actions spoke volumes of his love for his family and home.

173

In his last days he would tell his wife, Frances, to please put on his socks and shoes, because he was going home, even though he knew where he was all the time.

This home he was referring to is in God's Word. 2 Corinthians 4:16-18 and 5:1. (GNT).

For this reason we never become discouraged. Even though our physical being is gradually decaying, yet our spiritual being is renewed day after day. And this small and temporary trouble we suffer will bring us a tremendous and eternal glory, much greater than the trouble. For we fix our attention, not on things that are seen, but on things that are unseen. What can be seen lasts only for a time; but what cannot be seen lasts forever... For we know that when this tent we live in—our body here on earth, is torn down. God will have a house in heaven for us to live in, a home He himself made, which will last forever.

–Richard N. Summerford, Son-in-law

Carwell Haney

That Woman

I could feel my blood begin to boil.

March 31, 1995
Myrtle Beach, South Carolina

T he air was crisp and cool early that Friday morning. It was almost springtime, and Wanda and I had plans to attend a Christian ladies' retreat that weekend in Myrtle Beach. We were anxious and excited about going and had been busy packing all week.

Suddenly, my cell phone rang. It was Martha.

"Hey, hon, you and Wanda having fun packing to go to the beach?"

Even though we did not grow up together, I knew Martha well— and could tell by her voice that something was troubling her.

"Yep, we can hardly wait. What's wrong?"

"Well, guess what? I think I can come to join Wanda and you at the beach this weekend."

The tone in her voice had changed, and I could tell she was attempting to mask her true feelings.

"That would be great. What time do you expect to arrive?"

"Well, I'm at least three hours away. I imagine it will be about 7:00 p.m. when I get there."

"What's up, Martha? I know this isn't just a pleasure trip for you. Something important is going on. I can hear it in your voice."

"I really need to see you both because I have some big news, but I can't tell you now." Her voice softened. "I want to talk with you in person."

That night, the three of us gathered in a booth at a Shoney's restaurant near the beach.

We couldn't imagine what was going on. Wanda and I thought maybe she and Mickey were having marital problems.

Martha took a breath. I could sense she had something to talk to us about, but didn't know how to tell us.

Then she burst into tears.

"I've found our mother," she said softly, tears rolling down her cheeks.

Our mother? Her words shocked us.

We knew Martha had been searching for our birth mother a long time, but we seldom talked about it. All our lives, Wanda and I had heard conflicting stories about her. We were even told she'd died in a plane crash in Oklahoma many years ago.

I'd spent hours requesting documents from social services and obtained what they called "unidentifiable information." I didn't like a lot of what I read. From the paperwork, it appeared our biological mother, Bertha, had abandoned us and never looked back.

But where I had reservations and a lot of confusion, Martha seemed excited.

"I contacted a private investigator," she said, smiling through her tears. "And through his assistance, I've been able to locate her whereabouts."

I wasn't quite sure how Wanda would react, and I was very concerned for her, but she just sat there and listened.

"You found her?" Wanda asked gently.

Wanda and I had confided in each other that we were very concerned for Martha regarding our biological mother. We'd even discussed before, if she did find her, how Martha would handle the news.

Now she'd done just that.

My heart pounded. What if Bertha rejects her children once again? Would she be glad to hear Martha had searched for and found all of us?

Our dinner arrived, but we could only pick at the food.

"She called me yesterday. I have her number and she wants us to call her tonight so she can speak to each of us. Her name is Bertha Jordan Grimes," Martha began. "She's been married to the same gentleman for over twenty-seven years."

I couldn't resist a smirk. "So, what's her explanation for the cause of all of us being put in foster care?"

Martha sighed. "Well, her story is that she and all of us were being abused by our biological father. He drank heavily and he beat her, and possibly abused us, both physically and sexually."

I could feel my blood begin to boil. "I don't believe that. Wanda was only eight months old, and I would have been less than three years old." I couldn't imagine a man beating and abusing children that young.

"Bertha also says our father's brothers were raping her. She says his brothers would wait until she was pregnant, and then they'd take turns on her because that way they knew they couldn't father her child." She shook her head. "Whether all that's true or not, I don't really know."

"Well, answer me this. If we are babies and being abused by these men, how does a mother walk away and leave us there?" I gritted my teeth. "I don't believe a word of what she says. I'll go along with calling her if you want, but right now, all I know is what the court papers say. She left us tied up in a house, alone, because that's how they found us. Her excuses sound empty to me. I wouldn't know what to say to her."

I could hear the anger in my voice, and I took a deep breath.

"Look." I forced calm into my voice. "Let's at least make a list right now of questions we feel are appropriate to ask her. It's not the time to go into all this on the phone now."

"That's a great idea." Martha nodded.

It took a while that evening for us to muster the courage to dial Bertha's number. We each said our hellos and spoke with her for a few minutes. Bertha seemed to be crying, so her husband, James, took the phone from her and talked with us. He asked us about our families and our children.

Before we hung up, Bertha said she couldn't wait to meet everyone.

The call left me feeling unsettled, curious—and angry.

We decided to return to the retreat and share with the group about our experience. We asked for prayer because we planned to go to Lydia and share the news with Mama. Martha wanted to be the one to tell her. She wanted Mama to understand why she decided to search for her mother.

I was still angry at Martha for interrupting our weekend and Bertha for abandoning us.

That Sunday, my feet dragged as I walked into my Mama's house with Martha. Wanda and I sat quietly on the couch, and Martha sat close to Mama and began to share the news with her.

Mama listened and seemed genuinely happy for Martha.

"Don't worry about my feelings, Martha. I understand your wanting to find your mother."

Mama tried to assure Martha that everything would be all right.

"This certainly does not lessen my love for you, hon."

We spent the afternoon talking with Mama and having fun just being with her.

Later in the afternoon, Martha decided she had to leave to get home before dark. She kissed Mama and us goodbye and then left in her car.

Everything was different once again.

I felt completely out of sorts, like I had betrayed my mama.

I spent as much time as possible with Mama that day to reassure her that nothing had changed between us, that she was my "mama," and always would be.

Mama reassured us that she felt that way too. Still, I was worried.

#

May 25, 1995

Martha called to tell us that our birth mother was planning to come to South Carolina in July. At first, this was more unwelcome news for me. I struggled all week with what decision I should make. Should I meet Bertha? Would this too be a betrayal to my mama?

I knew I'd have to visit Mama and tell her Bertha would visit us. That, too, I dreaded.

Wanda and I planned to meet the next Sunday at Mama's to tell her about the reunion. Finally, late that afternoon, we worked up enough courage to tell her. Mama was upset at first. It was like she never wanted to hear anything more about her. But she took the news better than I had envisioned. She said she was glad we were not trying to hide anything from her. We assured her none of this would ever change our love and devotion to her.

"I'm just glad your Daddy isn't alive right now. He wouldn't be able to accept any of this. He'd always said, 'If that woman ever steps foot at my door, I'll blow her brains out!' I know he'd be heartbroken." I realized then that she, too, felt that way.

I didn't want to meet Bertha. And I told Mama that. I had nothing I wanted to say to her. Or rather, I knew she wouldn't want to hear what I had to say to her. Over these past few months, my anger hadn't waned.

Mama said she didn't want Wanda to go without me. If one of us went, she wanted both of us to go together.

After much pleading from Martha and Wanda, I decided I had to be with them that Friday to meet Bertha. Martha had located David after not having heard from him in a long time. He decided to come so all four children would be together again after more than thirty years of separation—together with the mother who'd abandoned us.

The long drive alone up I-26 toward Greer, where Martha lived, was more difficult for me than I had imagined it would be. I tried to distract my thoughts for a long time by singing along with the radio. At the Woodruff sign, I made the turn off the interstate and took the long country road all the way through town.

That's when it hit me.

I began to cry uncontrollably and caught myself asking Daddy in heaven not to be mad at me. I prayed for Mama to understand and not feel we were abandoning her.

By 9:15 p.m., I'd made it to Greer. I waited at the hotel, where I expected Wanda to meet me. She arrived at 10:15 p.m., and we called Martha. We were ready for her to come to meet with us.

Finally, at 11:45 p.m., we all walked down to the lobby where we met our biological mother for the first time in three decades.

Bertha hugged us all for a long time. When she wrapped her arms around me, I felt my spine stiffen. I did not want her touching me.

Martha insisted we take pictures, but I intentionally did not smile. This was no happy occasion for me.

Not knowing what kind of gift would be appropriate at a time like this, I'd brought a bouquet of flowers and Wanda brought her a Disney shirt.

She had no gifts for us.

Around 1:00 a.m., we realized none of us had eaten dinner. We shared our story with the hotel manager. Touched, he called his friend at Shoney's and asked the manager to keep the restaurant open a little longer. The Shoney's manager was excited and invited us over. He prepared a fresh breakfast just for us, his only customers at that late hour. We visited and took many more pictures until about 2:00 a.m.

Then, exhausted, we went our separate ways to rest for the evening.

Wanda and I roomed together that night at the hotel. Fuming, I grabbed an ice pack for my head. Wanda was much more forgiving than I and asked me to give Bertha a chance and see what happens next. We cried as we hugged until we fell asleep, emotionally exhausted.

Martha had planned a family reunion for the following day. Bertha would see her sisters and other relatives she'd not seen in years. We met cousins, uncles, and aunts we had never known.

After much visiting and eating, we returned to Martha's house to share with Bertha some pictures and memories of our childhood. My husband and children were meeting us there.

I'd been holding back my feelings all day, but now I started to feel excited. Sitting on the couch at Martha's, I eagerly slid out two photo albums of Mama's and asked Bertha if she would like to see how Wanda and I grew up. I loved those albums. There were many childhood pictures of our birthday celebrations and Christmases together. I thought it would make Bertha relieved or even joyful to see how happy her children had been.

But instead of sitting down beside us on the couch and looking at the pictures, Bertha stood and said something I'll never forget.

"No, I don't want to look at your pictures. You don't know how bad things were when you were little. I was being raped all the time by your father's brothers. I had no food to feed you children. Many times, there was only cornmeal and water in the house." She gritted her teeth and said, "I did the best I could."

"But you left us there!" I said a little louder than I ought.

Wanda and I stared at each other in disbelief. I closed the books. "I'm leaving!"

As I stood, Bertha turned her back to us and walked into the kitchen. Martha trailed behind.

When Martha came back in the room, she announced, "Bertha wants us to call her Mother."

That was it. I lost it.

"Seriously?" I shouted. "She does not even care about our childhood after she walked away and went on with her life, as if we never existed, and now she wants us to call her Mother? Unbelievable. No way. She is not my mother, nor my mom. Nothing. As my daddy said, she is 'that woman' named Bertha. That's all."

I was so angry I didn't even care if she heard me.

My children, now in their teens, were also beginning to get upset. They had not wanted to come to Greer to meet Bertha. They, too, felt like they were betraying their real grandmother. But I had insisted that they come to join in with all their other cousins on the momentous occasion, thinking it would be a happy one. I found out later that my youngest daughter, Lisa, called her real grandmother to come and get her. My mother drove all the way from Hartsville to Greer, picked up Lisa, and drove away.

After witnessing my burst of anger, we decided it was time for all of us to leave. Martha begged us to go outside as cordially as we could and take several more pictures with Bertha. You could look at our faces in the pictures and know this was not a happy occasion for any of us.

Finally, we gave our last hugs goodbye to Martha and Mickey, got in our cars, and sped away.

It was the first and last time I ever saw "that woman." She sent me one letter and one card for some occasion, but I never responded. She never asked for forgiveness. It was like she felt justified and less guilty after having met us.

It may have been resolved for her, but I was still angry that she had abandoned us and was acting like she did nothing wrong. Martha found comfort in a long-lost mother, but I felt differently. I always said, "I don't hate her. I have no feelings for a woman I do not know and will not pretend I do."

We never spoke again.

The Last Link

I got two good girls.

August 5, 2010
Lydia, South Carolina

Fifteen years later, I had been called home to be with Mama. I had been home for a week and wouldn't leave her side.

"Aunt Mary Lou," I quietly said when she answered the phone, "I need to tell you Mama is not doing well. The doctor is telling us she won't be with us much longer. You need to come to say your goodbyes."

"Oh, sweetheart." My aunt's voice was tender. "Thank you for calling me. I will come by tomorrow and see her."

Her caregiver, Brenda, had been helping me all morning making calls to all of Mama's sisters and her last living brother, Uncle Newt.

"Is that all of her sisters and brothers, dear?" Brenda asked as she rubbed my back.

"Yes, she had nine brothers and sisters, but only a few still remain."

Brenda headed toward the kitchen. "Let me make you girls some breakfast."

Her hands were shaking as she reached into the cabinet for the coffee filters. This was as hard on Brenda as it was on us. She had grown to love "Miss Lydia," a nickname she affectionately called her. Mama loved Brenda, too.

"I don't need a caregiver. I can take care of myself." Mama had argued with me the first time I'd mentioned looking for someone to stay with her during the day.

She'd always been independent and strong. She just didn't realize or want to accept her limitations.

As Mama's health declined, I called several caregivers and interviewed them. It was not until I spoke with Brenda that I felt comfortable with my decision. Her voice was reassuring. I knew immediately she was the right one.

I wasn't aware of it at first, but Mama remembered Brenda with much fondness. Brenda used to sit in front of Mama at Mt. Elon Baptist Church. She remembered how Mama was the first to welcome her as a new member visiting for the first time. Mama had leaned forward and patted Brenda's shoulder, saying, "Welcome." She did this every Sunday thereafter.

Mama would sit in her reserved seat every Sunday. When we visited, we'd always have to count the rows as we came in to be sure we were in the right pew. Row nine, middle section. We would lay our purses and hymn books out to save seats for the rest of the family. If we were off a row, we'd all have to move back or forward one row until we were properly seated.

Initially, as Brenda became Mama's caregiver, Mama wanted to show Brenda she could take care of herself. She would try to stand in the kitchen and cook. "Brenda, you just can't cook me what I want," she'd say, or think of difficult dishes just to test Brenda.

One day, Mama grinned from ear to ear. "Brenda, I want a mess of bream."

"A mess of bream?" Brenda laughed out loud. "What, pray tell, is a mess of bream?"

"See, I told you, you can't cook like me. Yes, I want me some bream. It's pronounced b-r-i-m and it's like crappie or bass. Now get on to the fish market. I like it fresh."

Brenda made the quick trip to the fish market and cooked bream for her supper.

"Yum! Brenda, I do believe this is the best bream I've ever tasted."

They loved each other from that day on. Mama became like a mother to Brenda.

Every Sunday, Mama would ask for a plate of food from Mr. B's next door to her house. Bobby and Reba Goff owned Mr. B's restaurant.

"Brenda, it's almost 11:30, you better call Reba and order our lunch."

"Yes, ma'am, right away."

As Brenda walked in the door to Mr. B's, Reba would hand Brenda the "to go" bag already wrapped tightly.

"Here you go, Brenda. I hope you and Ms. Frances enjoy your Sunday lunch. Please tell her hello for me. Now you put that money away. You know there's no charge for Ms. Frances."

"Thank you, Reba," Brenda smiled as she turned to leave. Brenda thought to herself that not many good folks are left in this world like Bobby and Reba Goff.

When Brenda returned from Mr. B's, she'd prepare Mama's plate and a glass of sweet tea on the table, then help Mama shuffle to her seat. Mama insisted on eating her meals at the table.

Mama loved to have her nails polished. "I need my nails polished today, Brenda. Just look how bad they are."

"I'll paint them for you as soon as we finish our lunch," Brenda would say. "I think you may have some company today. Linda and Wanda said they're coming by. And I think Debbie said she's stopping by, too."

"Good. I sure miss my girls, Brenda. And that Debbie keeps me in stitches."

One of my favorite memories of Mama was when I'd sit on the arm of her favorite gold chair, and Mama would say, "Scratch my back, Linda. No one can scratch it for me quite like you."

I'd smile and start to scratch her back.

"Over to the left … now right…." She giggled as I danced my fingers up and down, tickling her.

Her body had become frail, but one night Mama acted silly and started to try to dance. Her body was too weak to stand, so Brenda picked her up in her arms and they danced across the kitchen floor.

Since Mama could no longer attend church, Wanda stopped by the church every week to bring sermons on tape from the pastor. Mama would listen to them as she sat in her chair, eyes closed so she wouldn't miss a word and imagining herself sitting in the pew.

My cousin Debbie was an organist in her church, and she'd visit Mama almost weekly, making the long trip from Rock Hill and bringing along cassette tapes of herself playing hymns on the piano. Mama almost wore those tapes out, playing them over and over again.

Time passed quickly, and by summer, Brenda had been caring for Mama for several months.

"Brenda," Mama said one day while sitting in her lounge chair.

"Yes, Miss Lydia?"

"Take care of my girls for me, won't you? I worry about Wanda without me."

"I will, Mrs. Haney."

Brenda took Mama out on the screened porch every afternoon.

The warm summer breeze was soothing, and the sounds of the cars and trucks passing by almost sounded like waves of the ocean. As evening settled in, they'd listen to the cicadas and frogs singing in the distant trees.

"I feel closer to God out here," she'd said softly one night as they watched the sunset together.

That was the last night they would share stories on the porch. From then on, Mama lay in her hospital bed we'd set up in her bedroom. Hospice was called in to monitor her, and Brenda stayed by her side. Brenda called Martha, Wanda, and me to come home as she felt her time was drawing to a close. Three weeks passed, and Mama was in and out of a coma.

Wanda called her sons, Phillip and Jon. They came immediately and refused to leave that night.

Phillip was standing behind us around her bed, trying to hold in his tears and stay strong.

"You know, Pappy died on December 5," he said. "I bet Nanny is waiting until tomorrow to leave us so she and Pappy would both have died on the fifth of the month, don't you think?"

"I bet you're right, Phillip." I smiled at the sweet thought. "It would be just like her to do that."

That afternoon as Wanda and I sat at her bedside, Mama opened her eyes and said loudly, "I got two good girls."

Wanda and I stared at each other as if to say, "Did you just hear what I heard?"

We both jumped up and quietly went to her, each of us holding one of her hands.

"Mama, did you say something?" I softly asked.

"I got two good girls," Mama repeated, eyes closed.

Wanda and I smiled.

"Yes, but that's because we got a good Mama," I said.

Her eyes remain closed, but we noticed a sweet smile come across her face. No other words were ever spoken by Mama.

When I was alone in the room with Mama later that night, I rubbed her forehead and leaned down close by her ear.

"Don't worry, Mama. I promise I'll take care of Wanda for you. I always have, haven't I? I will take care of everything. You can go be with Daddy, Mama. I love you."

The hospice nurse, with the wonderful name of Angel, had been sitting by her bed all night, along with Brenda, monitoring her vital signs while helping to keep us all calm. No one wanted to sleep that night. We all felt it would be her last. Martha, Wanda, and I took turns going back into the living room to catch a short nap on the couch, insisting we were to be awakened at any sign.

I found myself glued to the chair next to Mama's bed. I watched her gown move up and down with each breath she took. As long as I could see her gown move, I knew her heart was still beating.

Suddenly, I saw the movement getting slower and slower.

I looked up at the nurse, and she calmly said, "Go get your sisters now."

Wanda had just fallen asleep after hours by Mama's bed.

"Wanda must be here, too, even though I hate to wake her up. I know she's tired, but she wants to be with her, too," Martha said.

"Yes," I nodded. "I hate to wake her, too, but I think this is it. Go get her."

Martha gently woke Wanda, and they rushed back to the bedroom.

Wanda, Martha, and I held Mama's hands when she took her last breath at 5:36 a.m.

"She is a beautiful lady with such a smooth copper complexion." The hospice nurse shared. "I can tell just by watching you three ladies that she was a great mother to you all."

"Yes, she sure is," I smiled as I looked at Wanda and Martha. "You know she always prayed that when her time came, she would go peacefully in her own home. I'm so thankful we were able to keep our promise to her. Thank you, Brenda."

We all put our heads down on Mama and softly sobbed.

The hospice nurse gently pulled us away. "Let me check her, please."

We all let go of Mama's hands and held onto each other as we stepped back.

"Yes, she's gone," the nurse said after putting the stethoscope to Mama's chest.

She looked at us with tears in her own eyes. She had grown close to our mother after sitting by her bed for days.

Trying to hold back their tears, Phillip and Jon left to go outside.

"What do we do now?" I asked.

The nurse gave us each a hug. "You all can go in the den and be together awhile. I'll make all the calls that need to be made."

We knew that we could not have made it through this process without the wonderful hospice nurses we'd had. The stress of handling everything by ourselves would have been too much.

Wanda, Martha, and I slowly walked down the hall, arm in arm, consoling each other through our tears. The last link to our old lives was gone. We only had each other now, the three sisters. For so many years, it had not been this way. But for now, we were together, yet alone.

The sun rose outside our windows as Mama left us to meet her Savior. How fitting. She was always up early every morning. She loved the sunrises and sunsets.

No words were spoken for a long time that morning. Martha made a fresh pot of coffee and put a few pieces of toast in the oven, trying to make sure we all ate something.

We were standing next to each other on the porch when they rolled Mama out on the gurney. But my feet felt heavy, like I had concrete blocks on them. I couldn't move.

We stood, arm in arm, watching as they wheeled her out of the house and into the long, black hearse and drove away with our Mama.

#

The next few days were a blur. Most of the arrangements had already been made, and I checked my list of things to do before the funeral.

One evening, Wanda and I cleaned out her bedroom and sat down to go through the antique cedar chest Mama kept at the foot of her bed.

It's the same cedar chest Wanda and I always wanted to rummage through as children, but it'd been locked for years. We were never allowed to look in it. When we were children, we had many failed attempts to see what was inside. And yet that night I held the key in my hand.

The key was small and worn and was the last key on Mama's key ring. The strange feeling of opening something she'd kept secret for so long made me feel guilty.

I took a deep breath. Here we were, staring into our past.

Slowly we knelt before the chest. I opened the lid, and the smell of cedar filled my nose. The chest was neatly filled with papers and other items. First, we found simple things, a few old Christmas placemats, paid bills, and bank statements from years past. We looked at pictures of Daddy from his twenty-nine years at Sonoco Products Company. One showed him standing next to J.L. Coker Sr., as Daddy was presented with plaques for his many years of service to the company. We found Mama's beautiful photo albums safely tucked away with pictures of her grandchildren.

My eyes filled. "I wonder if after Daddy passed away and Mama was alone in the house, did she ever kneel down and browse through her cedar chest?"

"I'm sure she did." Wanda sniffed.

I handed her a tissue and we continued searching.

Hot tears rolled down my cheeks as I read a letter J.L. Coker Sr. sent my grandfather, V.C. Elmore Sr., my mama's father, who'd been chief of police. The handwritten letter encouraged my grandfather to believe his act of heroism was admirable when he had to shoot a criminal in order to save someone's life. It made me feel so proud of my heritage.

At the bottom of the chest we found old brown envelopes with information from the South Carolina Department of Social Services—papers from our adoption. Wanda and I had known since childhood that we were adopted, so this came as no real surprise to us, although it was very special to actually see the court orders.

I slowly ran my fingers across the original signatures of Frances and Carwell Haney and imagined them smiling at each other as they signed the papers.

Beneath the papers, something else caught my eye.

"Wanda, look. What's in these small white boxes?"

"I can't imagine. Be careful, they look fragile."

We peeled back the tissue paper, now yellow with age, and found two small dresses. One was a thin blue dress, and the other was even smaller with pink and blue plaid.

"Wanda, do you think these could be the dresses we wore home on our first day here?"

"They have to be—look how tiny they are!"

We hugged each other tightly and cried for a long time.

Everything went perfectly at her funeral as scheduled. Mama's "going away celebration" was beautiful. Her casket was pretty—silver with pink roses. We had gone to Mitchell's Florist and chose flowers for the spray on top, as well as other flowers. The Mitchells, too, were close friends of Mama's, and they helped us pick out only the best for her.

August 8, 2010 was the day we said our final goodbyes to our wonderful mother. All her family had come—her brothers, sisters, grandchildren, and great-grandchildren, along with many other friends and relatives—to show their final respects to this extraordinary lady. Her obituary was a fitting tribute to the special lady she was.

From The State newspaper:

Frances Olivia Elmore Haney, 88, went to be with her Lord on Thursday, August 5, 2010. She passed away at her home in Lydia, SC. Frances was the widow of Carwell Haney.

Funeral services will be held at 2 p.m. on Sunday, August 8, 2010, at Mt. Elon Baptist Church with burial in the church cemetery. The Rev. Rob Brazzell, the Rev. Robin King, and the Rev. Tom Faucette will officiate. The family will receive friends from 5:00 to 7:00 p.m. Saturday, August 7, 2010, at Brown-Pennington-Atkins Funeral Home. Memorials may be made to Mt. Elon Baptist Church, Box 38, Lydia, SC 29079 or to Child Evangelism Fellowship of SC, Box 211084, Columbia, SC 29221.

Born in Lee Co., SC, she was a daughter of Hartsville's former Chief of Police, the late Vernon Carl Elmore, Sr., and the late Elise Mathis Elmore. She was a long-time member of Mt. Elon Baptist Church and a charter member of West Hartsville Baptist Church. She was very active in the A. Josey Sunday School Class and with the homebound. She retired from Dixie's Federal Credit Union after twenty-four years of service. Frances was a devoted mother, grandmother and great-grandmother

*and was affectionately known to all as "Granny Frances." The
family would like to express their gratitude for the excellent
care provided by Harmony Care Hospice and especially her
"Angel" and a special "thank-you" to her wonderful caregiver,
Brenda Roberts.*

*Surviving are her daughters Linda (Richard) Summerford, of
Chapin, SC; Wanda Hatley of Lydia, SC; grandchildren Jenni-
fer Lynn Summerford of Columbia, SC, Lisa S. (Kevin) Kyzer of
Chapin, SC, Phillip Hatley of Hartsville, SC, Jonathan (Melissa)
Hatley of Cheraw, SC; great-grandchildren Aydin Quick, Averi
Quick, Leland Bateman, Becca Howle, Brittney Howle; broth-
ers V.C. (Mildred) Elmore Jr. of Hartsville, SC, Newt (Shirley)
Elmore of Rock Hill, SC; sisters Mary Lou Gregory of Union,
SC, Doris (Benny) Rowe of West Palm Beach, FL; special
daughter, Martha Kennemore of Greenville, SC, and her children, Sherri (Jason) Forrester and Shane (Kala) Kennemore;
numerous nieces and nephews.*

*She was preceded in death by her brother, Charles Elmore;
sisters, Mattie Mathis, Lucille Lane, Loretta Rhodes.*

I took the two little dresses and had them put into shadow boxes.
Carl Pennington at the funeral home found us two easels, and the
dresses were beside Mama's casket with notes below them describing
their meaning. I watched and smiled as we stood in the receiving line
while people put their hands to their mouths and gasped as they read
the descriptions.

After the service, we all went back to Mama's house and sat in the
den sharing funny stories and memories about Mama.

That's when someone in the room said something that shocked us
to our core.

"You do know that Frances was married before, don't you?" I turned my head around to listen more carefully. "And that she had a baby."

I had to find the nearest armchair to sit down. I was dizzy and suddenly thought I was going to faint.

"What did you just say?" I looked around the room with a look of disbelief on my face.

Wanda was standing and she too looked for a chair to sit in.

Everyone had been talking at once, but suddenly the room got quiet and we repeated our question.

"What did you say? Mama was married before our daddy and had a baby? That's not true. She told us that the reason she adopted us was because she could not have children."

"Yes, it's true," Aunt Mary Lou slowly nodded her head. "She was married to a man before your father, and she had a baby, but it was stillborn. She had moved to Louisiana with her husband, but after the baby died, she was unhappy and wanted to return home. My daddy and Uncle V.C. went to get her and brought her home."

Of all the things I anticipated this day, this news was certainly not one of them.

I stared at everyone. There were all nodding their heads.

My cousin, Jeannette said, "Yes, it's true."

It seemed like everyone else in the room knew this information about our mother, yet Wanda and I had no idea.

How could she have kept this secret from us all these years? Why had she never told us?

I was shaking in disbelief. I could not reconcile this news in my mind or heart.

"What else can you tell me about this?" I asked, searching the group for answers.

"That's about all we know. We were about ten years younger than her, so we didn't really know what all happened."

No one mentioned it anymore that day.

This news would have to wait for another time. For now, I had to take care of her estate and make much more difficult decisions.

Just a Box of Ashes

I suppose God kept me from burying his ashes because he was sending you here to get them.

May 7, 2011
Linda

Six months later, I was just beginning to come up for air after the grief of losing my mother. One night, just before 11:00 p.m., my cell phone rang. It was my sister, Martha.

Something must be wrong. She's usually in bed by now since she goes to work early each morning.

I grabbed my cell phone, "Hello. Martha?"

Her voice was soft. "Hi, hon. Hope I didn't wake you."

"No, we're still up. What's wrong?"

"Hon, I'm sorry to tell you this, but I believe our brother, David, might be dead."

"Dead?" I could barely speak the word.

A wave of dizziness washed over me. We had not heard from our brother in over two years. He had become very reclusive and distant to each of us. We sent him letters and cards, but never received a response.

"Yes. His ex-wife called me out of the blue last night and said a collection agency reached out about a bill that was past due. If it was not paid immediately, they were going to place a claim against David's estate. That's when she suspected—why else would they say something about his estate unless he's dead? How can we find out for sure? Who do we call?"

By that time, I was sitting in front of my computer. "Well, let's start by looking up funeral homes in Easley, since that's the last place we know he lived."

But nothing came up.

"I'll try to get more information tomorrow. You get some sleep. Love you," Martha said as she hung up.

I couldn't go to bed then. I was wide awake, wondering if my brother was gone.

I returned to the computer and again clicked on one of the places in Easley, Robinson Funeral Home. For some reason, I kept going back to that funeral home, searching. Finally, I entered only the last name in my search—Jordan.

One click of the mouse changed everything.

There were six names listed. I read down the list. Number five: *William David Jordan, age 59.*

My heart thumped. My eyes couldn't move.

I clicked on his name.

William David Jordan, age 59, husband of the late Cindy Thrasher Jordan, passed away on March 26, 2010, at St. Francis Hospital. Plans will be announced by Robinson Funeral Home.

I read it over and over. My hand finally found my cell phone again, and I called Martha back.

"I found it, Martha."

I told her where to find it, and she read it out loud with me in disbelief. There was no full obituary, only that short blurb.

"Look at the date," I said. "March 26, 2010—that was over a year ago! Martha, the names of his family are nowhere to be seen. His sisters, whom he had not seen for over forty years but had been miraculously found, are not even mentioned!"

Who would have done that? Did he do that deliberately? We could not understand. None of his family was mentioned, not parents or us. It was as if we'd never existed to him.

"What do we do now?" Martha's voice cracked.

"I'll go to the funeral home tomorrow." The plan was formulated in my mind as I spoke. I knew Martha couldn't get off work on such short notice. "We need to tell Wanda, but this isn't something I can tell her over the phone."

The next morning, on just a few hours of sleep, I got in my car and headed for my baby sister's home in Lydia. It was only seventy-five miles to Wanda's house, but the drive seemed to take hours.

Finally, I arrived at her doorstep. I rang her bell. From behind the door, I heard her little dog, Peanut, barking.

No answer.

I rang the bell again. Nothing.

I called her cell phone.

"Come to the door, Sis," I said when she answered. "I'm here."

"No, you're not." She laughed.

"Yes, I am."

A moment later, I could hear the sound of the door unlocking. It swung open, and there she stood, fear in her eyes.

"What's wrong? Something must be bad for you to just show up on my doorstep."

"Let's sit down."

We sat on her living room couch and I told her the news.

Then, simultaneously, we blurted, "We have to go to Easley today."

Thirty minutes later, we were driving in my car across the state, headed toward Easley.

Questions swirled. How did it happen? Who was with him? Was he alone? If he got sick, why didn't he call us, or why didn't someone call us? But we were unable to come up with any answers.

The funeral director stood in the doorway as we asked him all our questions, the bulging file on our brother in his hands. The end of my brother's life was in that folder. I couldn't imagine why he had so much information on David. What was written in them?

"I have several funerals today, so I don't have much time," he said. "I can show you several things in here. The death certificate is public record, so you can have a copy of it. You'll see that a lady listed there, who called herself his friend, is the one who came to the funeral home to make arrangements for him. He was cremated."

"Cremated?" I put my hand over my mouth, realizing how loud I was.

"Yes, ma'am. I suppose she didn't know what to do since she was unaware he had a family."

The director tried to console us, but Wanda and I shook our heads in disbelief.

"Where is he buried?" Wanda asked.

"I don't know, but my paperwork says he'd planned to be buried at Hopewell Baptist Church in Seneca. I suppose you could see if the lady buried him there." The funeral director looked uncomfortable. "You see, his friend only paid for the cremation and wasn't willing to pay for the rest of the funeral services. So, we just gave her his remains. At that point, it was her responsibility to bury him."

"Thank you for your time." We shook hands with him and slowly began to walk away.

"I am so sorry for your loss," we heard him say.

After we got into the car, we looked at the death certificate.

"There's the name of his friend who made the arrangements, Daniele Stephens."

Who was she, and why was she closer to our brother than we? How could we have let this happen?

For a long time, Wanda and I sat in the car in stunned silence. We vowed then that we would never lose touch.

We headed down a long country road next to Seneca, and Hopewell Baptist Church.

The church was on a hill with a large veranda on the front. Wanda and I got out of the car and searched for the front door, finally locating a sign that said, "Ring Bell."

"Come on in out of the heat." A kind lady greeted us. "How may I help you today?"

"We have a rather strange request of you." I told her about our search.

She turned to pick up some large albums. "Let me see if we have a plot with the name Jordan on it."

She searched the books, but there was no plot with the name Jordan.

The lady gave us a sympathetic smile. "Are you sure this is the right church?"

"No, not really," I said, "but there are other Hopewell Baptist churches in the area. So, we'll continue to look."

"I hope you find your brother," she said as Wanda and I turned to walk away.

"Thank you. We do too."

Deflated, we sat in the car a moment.

"I felt sure that was the right church. Where to next, Wanda?"

She shook her head. "I don't know where to go from here."

"Let's look at that death certificate again. Didn't the funeral director say the lady's name and address were on it?"

"Yes, there's her address right there, see? Number 217."

We both looked at the GPS.

"Put the address in, and let's see if we can find it. I'm not leaving here today until we find David."

We followed the directions for several miles. Suddenly, the GPS told us to turn left.

"Hey, this looks like a pretty nice neighborhood. I suppose that's about David's speed." I giggled. "He liked lonely, wealthy ladies."

We rode around and around, checking numbers on the mailboxes and houses—215, 216, 218, 219, but no 217.

"Wouldn't that be our luck?" I turned the car around in the cul-de-sac. "Wait a minute. Here's a house with no number on it."

"But it looks abandoned. The grass and shrubs are all overgrown. No one could live here," Wanda said.

"But there's a car in the driveway." I pointed.

Walking up to the house, I noticed it looked like no one had cut the grass in over a year, and the shrubs were to the top of the windows. Who could live like this?

I knocked. Suddenly, I heard movement inside.

The front door opened. "Hello," said a teenage girl.

"Is this Number 217? Is Daniele Stephens' home?"

"Mom, someone's at the door for you!" The girl yelled toward the den and walked away.

A pale, sad-looking lady shuffled to the door. She seemed older than her years.

"I'm Daniele Stephens." She took a puff on her cigarette.

I could feel Wanda's eyes on me from the car. "My name is Linda. I am David Jordan's sister."

I looked deep into her eyes as I said my brother's name.

Daniele looked even more pale then and grasped the door as if she was about to faint.

"What? I didn't know he even had a sister."

"He has three sisters."

"Please, come in. We have a lot to talk about." She shook her head and welcomed me in.

I motioned to Wanda in the car to follow me inside. This was the place. Of all the houses in Easley, we came directly to the right one.

The house reeked with odor, mostly cigarette smoke. She lit a long cigarette as we sat on the couch. A large ashtray full of cigarette butts sat in the center of the coffee table.

"David and I met at the pizza restaurant just down the road. I was sitting alone one day, and he was sitting alone facing me. I suppose he could tell I was sad, so he came over to talk with me." Daniele began explaining her relationship to our brother.

Wanda and I looked at each other and nodded.

She took another puff. "We talked a long time, and I told him about all I was going through. He told me about his cancer. See, I'm just now getting to a point where I can even have a conversation with someone like this. I've been a basket case for about two years. You see that picture on the armoire there?"

She pointed a shaky finger.

"That's my thirteen-year-old daughter. She was killed in a car wreck back in 2009, and it almost killed me trying to deal with it. David was there for me many times. They wouldn't even let me see my daughter. She was badly burned beyond recognition. Shortly after her death, I was in a bad wreck myself and severely injured my back. It took months of rehab to even walk again. David would come and take me to my doctor appointments when my husband couldn't."

I frowned, confused. "So, you and David weren't a couple?"

"Oh, no, our friendship was nothing like that. I'm married!" She held up her left hand to show us her wedding band. "My husband works at the post office. Many times, he couldn't get off work, so David volunteered to take me to my appointments, and then I'd pay him back by taking him to his doctor appointments and treatments for his lung cancer. See that golden urn there on the mantle? Those are my daughter's ashes. I had to have her cremated. I couldn't bring myself to bury her, so I keep her memory alive, here with me."

Almost as an afterthought, she pointed again toward the armoire. "Oh, and by the way, David's remains are right there. In that drawer."

"What?" Wanda and I said simultaneously.

"Yes." She lit another cigarette. "The funeral home gave his remains to me. I couldn't decide what to do with them. I couldn't get up the courage or strength to bury him, either. I suppose God kept me from doing that because He was sending you here to get them."

Wanda reached over and took my hand. Neither of us could speak.

Daniele continued, "That's why my house looks like this. I haven't had any desire to clean or anything. Like I said, I'm surprised that we can even have this conversation. I'm usually hiding away in bed, waiting for each day to pass with no real desire to live. But I do have three other children to live for. Here's one of my daughters, Susan."

The teenager who'd answered the door had drifted into the room by then, and she perched by Daniele's side on the sofa. The girl smiled at us and held her mother's hand.

"I have another daughter who lives away and a son in the military. Their pictures are on the mantle. And here are David's remains. I suppose I can just give them to you now, so he can have a proper burial."

Daniele opened the doors at the bottom of the armoire and took out a small cardboard box.

Wanda and I stood as she handed the box to us. No beautiful urn. My brother's ashes were in a cardboard box!

"I think I need to call my sister, Martha, and tell her to come over here, too, and talk with you. Would that be okay?"

Daniele nodded, and I walked outside to call Martha and give her directions.

Martha was there within minutes.

"She's a basket case, Martha. I think we need to be kind and sensitive to this lady.

I explained to Martha about her losing her daughter and her own injuries from a car accident.

"She is just now able to sit and talk with anyone, so we must be careful with her. The main thing is that we leave here with David's remains. We don't know her, and this may be the only time we ever see her." I hugged Martha and we turned back toward the house.

"You're right." Martha and I walked arm in arm inside.

I introduced Martha to Daniele. She began to ask questions of Daniele, and we sat for another hour as she went into more details about their relationship. She again assured Martha that their relationship was just as friends. David was a kind man who had much empathy for others.

Finally, we thanked Daniele for her kindness shown to our brother. With the box of ashes in my hands, I assured her that she would most definitely be invited if we had a memorial service.

The three of us drove to a nearby restaurant and talked for a long time about what to do next. We determined we must bury him. The only question was at which graveyard and which church.

The next few days were a blur. I tried to focus at work, but I was distracted. I had to decide what to do about David's burial.

I remembered David had said he was in the navy, so the next day, I went to the naval office in Columbia on my lunch hour. I wasn't sure my brother was eligible for a flag presentation, but if he was, I wanted to honor him that way.

"Oh, yes, ma'am," the receptionist said. "I see here he was honorably discharged even though he did not serve very long. He is still eligible to have a flag presentation at his memorial service."

"Oh, that would be great!"

I couldn't believe it. At least that would be something special we could do.

Later that day, I received a call from a naval officer.

"We will have three or four naval officers there at the church during the funeral, and they will present a flag to someone in the family, and one of the officers will play 'Taps,'" he explained without hesitation.

And it was all free. I was shocked—and grateful.

I began to think of other things I could do for the service. I didn't want to make too much of it, but still I wanted it to be special for him. We set a date for May 14, 2011.

I typed up an obituary and laminated it on a card with his picture at the top. One of them I mailed to Daniele Stephens with a card of appreciation, inviting her to the service.

The next day, I received a call from the nice lady at Hopewell Baptist Church, the one we'd met that day on our discovery trip.

She sounded apologetic.

"After talking with you that day, I couldn't get you off my mind. I went out in the graveyard and just walked around, looking for your brother's name. And—I found it. He does have a plot!"

"What?"

"Yes, ma'am. I'm so sorry, but when you were here, I was looking for Jordan, but the plot is actually in the name of his wife, Cindy. She died just about a year ago of cancer, and her family had bought two plots—one for her and one for David." She rushed on. "It's quite a nice plot, actually. I hope you'll be able to come back and see it soon."

"Oh, goodness! We're actually planning a memorial service for David on May 14—this weekend."

She gave me the pastor's number, and I called him. Unfortunately, he was unavailable to preach David's service.

Everything else came together so perfectly. Why it happened the way it did was a mystery to us all, but we were grateful. We wanted to do everything we could to remember our brother with honor.

My husband could not attend the memorial service with us because of a work commitment, so I asked my pastor, the Rev. Noble Kendall, to say a few words about him.

I called Pastor Noble to explain my need and the situation. When I finished, I could tell he was holding back tears.

"Of course, Linda. I'll rearrange my schedule, and I'll be there for you. I can bring my guitar and sing a couple of songs if you like."

The day of the service, Wanda and I drove together to Seneca.

When we arrived, we parked at the back of the church, searching for his plot. It was beautiful with lots of gravel rocks and a large headstone. All we'd have to do was engrave the date of his death.

We drove to the front of the church, where we saw Martha, Pastor Noble, and three naval officers. The officers were all dressed in their navy uniforms and looked so nice and professional. My heart soared in gratitude.

Excited, we jumped out of the car to hug Martha and thank Pastor Noble for coming—and as we shut the car doors, all the doors locked.

We'd locked the keys in the car along with our camera, our purses, and David's flag.

I burst into tears.

One of the naval officers came up just then and put a comforting hand on my shoulder.

"It's okay, ma'am. We always bring an extra flag with us."

I couldn't believe it—what if he hadn't brought an extra one? We would not have been able to have the flag presentation. I felt that was confirmation that God was in control and always a step ahead of me.

It began to rain, so we dashed to the veranda of the church. Pastor Noble got out his guitar, and the naval officers began to run through a practice of the program. I watched in amazement. The storm rolled in all around us, but we hardly even noticed. We stood silently waiting for the service to begin.

We'd decided to let the flag be presented to Wanda, since she's the youngest. When the time came for the flag presentation, Wanda was clearly touched and began to cry.

I held my feelings in until the officer played "Taps." That's when I couldn't hold it in any longer—I sobbed quietly.

The pastor said a few sweet words of encouragement and read passages of Scripture to us. We really didn't know where David had stood in his relationship with God. We wondered whether he'd had a death-bed experience, or maybe spoken with a chaplain about his salvation in the hospital. We did not know. All we could do was hope.

But Pastor Noble knew exactly which verses of Scripture to use to comfort us. He strummed his guitar softly and sang two hymns beautifully, "Rock of Ages" and "Amazing Grace." He asked us to sing the other verses of "Amazing Grace" with him.

After the closing prayer, we said our goodbyes to the naval officers and snapped a few pictures of them with our cell phones so we would never forget their kindness and respect.

Then we all went to the gravesite and buried David's ashes. Each of us took turns shoveling gravel over the ashes. We spread the rocks and closed the plot.

I'd brought a small flag, and I put it close to the flowers someone had already left earlier for Cindy, for Mother's Day. Silently, we stood a few minutes, hugging each other.

We knew we would remember this moment forever.

After AAA unlocked my car, the three sisters went to a restaurant close by to get a bite to eat. Then Wanda and I headed back home while Martha drove away on her motorcycle.

Things were different now. We no longer had a big brother in our lives.

But we were relieved we had each other to comfort.

When I got back home, I emailed a copy of the obituary I'd made for David and sent it to Robinson Funeral Home to be posted on the funeral home's website. David now had an obituary, as it should be.

William David Jordan, 60, of Easley, SC, passed away on March 26, 2010, at St. Francis Hospital in Greenville, S C. He is the son of the late William Patrick Jordan, of Greenville,

SC, and Bertha Elizabeth Jordan Grimes, of Greenville, SC. David was born April 2, 1950, in Greenville, SC. He was the husband of the late Cynthia Jordan, of Easley, SC. He served in the U. S. Navy. David is survived by three sisters, Martha J. Kennemore (and the late Mickey Kennemore), of Greer, SC; Linda H. Summerford (Richard) of Chapin, SC; and Wanda H. Hatley, of Hartsville, SC; and many nieces and nephews. A graveside memorial service was held Saturday, May 14, 2011, at Hopewell Baptist Church, Seneca, SC.

On Independence Day, since my brother was a veteran, I thought it fitting to make a trip to Seneca and put flowers on his grave. It was a holiday, so most of the florists and other businesses were closed. I rode around Seneca in search of a florist.

The sign on the door to the last florist said "closed," but I could see a lady inside sitting at a table arranging flowers. I parked and walked to the door.

"Hi," I waved to the lady behind the window. She smiled and walked toward me.

"I know your sign says closed, ma'am, but I wondered if you'd be so kind as to let me purchase that beautiful arrangement I see in the window. I'd like to put it on my brother's gravesite today in honor of Independence Day."

I could see she was busy, but she took her time and unlocked the door for me. "Sure, hon, come on in. Which one is it?"

"That red, white, and blue arrangement. I thought it would be perfect for my brother, David."

"He must have been an important man in your life for you to go to so much trouble. Where are you from, anyway?"

"I've driven here from Columbia. I couldn't let the day go by without remembering my brother."

She got the arrangement. "What's the story behind that? I feel like there's a good story there."

"It's a long story, but we were separated as toddlers and able to be reunited a few years ago. He had a hard life growing up in foster care. He deserves to be honored today."

"Oh, my. I'm so glad I opened my door to you today. This is one of those God moments, isn't it?"

We smiled at each other.

I handed her the money and noticed an open Bible sitting on the table by the register.

"Yes, ma'am, I do believe it is."

I was still smiling as I reached over the counter and gave this stranger a big hug. Then I turned and proudly walked out the door with my beautiful red, white, and blue flowers for my brother.

Before I got in the car, I looked up at the bluest sky I think I'd ever seen. "I know that was you, God. Thank you."

WILLIAM DAVID JORDAN

Please join us for

A graveside memorial service

To remember the life of

William David Jordan

Saturday, May 14, 2011

3:00 P.M.

Hopewell Baptist Church

Seneca, South Carolina

The Cedar Chest

Today would be a hard day.

Fall, 2011
Lydia, South Carolina
Linda

"Home," I whispered as I drove. Today would be a hard day.

Last week it had seemed that autumn was far off, but now as I put my foot to the pedal, I noticed the leaves had started to change colors. I stuck my hand out the window. A chill danced through my fingers. I found it funny that even as an adult, I was amused as I glided my hand like a bird in the wind. I followed the long country roads. The beautiful fields of corn and cotton guided me home.

There was the natural artesian wellspring where families had stopped to fill their jugs with refreshing ice-cold water. My daddy loved to take us there to stand on the rocks and lean over, drinking straight from the fountain. He told us it had healing powers.

I rounded the curve toward the white church with two steeples, and I knew home was just a moment away. The church seemed small from a distance, but the memories it held for me were vast. The steps leading into the church echoed the sounds of baptisms, weddings, birth announcements, and funerals. The sun reflecting off the stained-glass windows sent a magnificent array of colors into the sky. From the inside, I always envisioned heaven through those windows.

But going home today would not be heaven for me. Today was our final visit to the house, when we'd get the remaining items and clean the house before putting it up for sale.

The sweet smell of magnolias filled the air and passed me by carelessly, yet haunting me. Slowly, I drove to the back of the church. I saw the gravesite where Mama peacefully rested in her eternal sleep beside Daddy, and my emotions hit me like a brick.

Slowly I got out of the car. I put silk flowers on her grave. I stood still for a moment, at a loss for words. Finally, I was able to speak, "I love you, Mama."

I wiped tears from my cheeks. Then I got back into my car and drove away.

Glancing to my right I saw the green, rolling hills come alive. It was Sunday, and with fall welcoming, Southern men took to the greens. I could hear the golf carts buzzing around, heading for the next hole. Pastels, khakis, and ball caps dressed the greens, like cotton candy on sticks ready to eat. The greens that now carry these new memories of Sundays once carried all of mine.

Our original home, with its old charm, still stood at the end of the long dirt road, tucked away from the Sunday golfers. That house where it all began for me—where my life really began.

I could almost see the old farm, the cows in the pasture, and another pasture beyond with those dreaded mules I hated. I envisioned my daddy plowing the fields.

One more curve and I'd be there.

Slowly I pulled into the driveway. I saw the yard was a bit overgrown and the hedges needed to be trimmed. I made a mental note, "Call Shug." He'd been Mama's gardener for years, especially when she became sick and couldn't keep it up anymore. I laughed, thinking of her at eighty, riding her Monroe lawn mower, cutting the grass and pulling up weeds in her flower bed. She'd seemed invincible.

Since Mama's passing, it was emotionally hard for Shug to come here. He and Mama had become dear friends. The last time he came, I brought him a glass of cold water and caught him tearing up as he pulled weeds among her flowers. He was proud and embarrassed that I'd noticed him wiping his face with his sleeve. I'd decided to send him home.

The crackling rocks scattered between my tires. I stopped to check the mail and saw crumpled papers overflowing the mailbox. I was not yet ready to see her name on the envelopes, to speak of her in the past. I decided to leave the mail in the box until later.

The old house hadn't changed much in all the years. The beautiful home had survived hurricanes, hailstorms, and dry, hot summers in the country. I'd loved sitting on the rounded brick steps watching the sunsets with my daddy.

It was pecan-picking time, and all the pecans were fresh and falling off the trees. Daddy had planted five pecan trees many years ago. Each tree had grown tall, stretching to the sky and providing shade from the Southern heat. In an attempt to avoid crushing the pecans, I made a loop around the drive. I could almost hear Mama say, "Linda, don't you run over my pecans, now."

I parked in the front by the porch steps and cracked the windows.

Will this be my last time here?

Closing my eyes, I took it all in—the drive, the flashbacks of the past, leading me here. To this moment.

"Lord, give me strength."

Stepping out of the car, the delicious smells of Mr. B's Seafood Restaurant next door filled my senses, and my stomach ached for some scrumptious down-home country cooking. I could almost taste the butter-soaked baby lima beans and juicy fried chicken. I was not the only one who was hungry. I glanced over and saw the herd of Sunday churchgoers, lining up for a good ole' Southern meal. If I could eat, I would be on my second helping of collard greens and cornbread. But not today.

Next door to Mr. B's was Tommy's Grocery. Mama loved Tommy's hot dogs with chili. She cried the day Tommy died suddenly of a heart attack. He was in his store that he loved when God called him home. I remembered how, growing up, we'd go there and fill little brown bags with an assortment of candies costing five cents each. We'd get an ice-cold Pepsi or Red Rock and wander down to the railroad tracks behind our house. The rails were hot under our feet, but we could walk for miles. I laughed at the thought. I don't remember ever wearing shoes except on Sundays. My collection of railroad nails was in my closet until Daddy found them.

"Now, Linda, those weren't yours to take," he'd said. The next day I put them all back.

The porch door creaked, and I got my pen and pad out again.

Fix porch door.

There would be plenty to repair before we put the house on the market.

Holding Mama's favorite key chain with the familiar blue leather band, I unlocked the door. It was stuck. It had been for years, and I could almost hear Mama say, "Pull up and put your hip into it. That's the only way to get it open." The laughter came bursting off my lips as I rolled my eyes and opened the door.

The air was musty and hot as if the walls were sweating. The faint sweet smell of her perfume lingered through the odors of sickness and sadness.

I walked around the empty house. I felt so alone. Slowly, I wandered each empty room, my mind filled with visions of the past. I could still see my bedroom with the beautiful cotton curtains made by Mama's hands. I missed my old radio on the nightstand where I'd listened to the Top 40 hits every night, lying at the foot of my bed with the cool breeze blowing on my face.

"Goodnight, God," I would always say after my prayers as I looked up at the full moon.

Next, I went into Mama and Daddy's bedroom. The four-poster bed and dresser had already been given to Wanda. She'd always loved that bedroom suite.

Only the rocking chair my grandmother had rocked us in, and Mama's beautiful antique cedar chest remained in the house.

Wanda arrived, and we walked around the house to be sure nothing was left in the closets or cabinets. I had left the vacuum cleaner at the house the last time I was there, along with some cleaning supplies. It was hard to do, but I ran the vacuum throughout the house, and we cleaned the bathrooms and kitchen counter thoroughly. We wanted it spotless before we advertised it.

I returned to my van with the vacuum and supplies, lifting out the dolly that I needed to help us lift the cedar chest.

Carefully, we loaded the chest and then Grandma's rocking chair, my most treasured gifts.

Before I got into the van, Wanda and I walked to the front of the house and just stood there. Remembering.

"Goodbye," I whispered as we held hands. "Thanks for the wonderful memories from our childhood. We will miss you, Beautiful Home."

Carwell and Frances Haney - 1983

The bond between my sisters and me is woven strong and will never be broken. Braided rope was used in the beginning of our lives to cause us harm, but we are not victims, we are overcomers.

God's Word affirms that we go through suffering so we can minister to and encourage others who are suffering (2 Corinthians 1:4). I truly believe God has called me to be a voice and an advocate to help prevent the next generation of foster children from falling through the cracks of a broken system.

The End

" ... A cord of three strands is not quickly broken."

Ecclesiastes 4:12

Dresses Linda and Wanda wore home on day of adoption
August 15, 1958

Epilogue

"Why didn't you want me? What was wrong with me?"

Recently I heard an actor ask those two questions during an interview. Ben Vereen, the well-known Broadway performer, said he was in his twenties when he discovered he had been adopted, and it had shaken him to his core. There he was on national TV at sixty-nine years old, still holding back tears.

These same questions come to the surface with any foster or adopted child. We take on guilt that is not ours. It's a feeling that will follow us throughout our lives and reveal itself in most relationships. I feel it myself many times, especially on my birthday. I never even thought about it growing up. I felt so much love and acceptance in my family that it made me feel all the more special. It was only after meeting our biological mother that the questions began to haunt me.

I am thankful I was removed from that horrible situation and, by God's sovereignty, given another chance at life. I have contemplated many times how terrible my life could have been had God not rescued me. I would not have wanted to grow up in extreme poverty. I am sure Wanda and I would have different personalities today—if we'd even survived.

I am grateful every day of my life that God intervened and gave Wanda and me another calling in life. I don't know why He did, but I am so thankful. Maybe our purpose is to share our story with others who were adopted, to let them know nothing is wrong with them— every child is special. I have come to realize that not only were my parents a gift to me, but *I* was a gift to them.

#

"You wove evil, but God rewove it together for good."

From You'll get Through This, video by Max Lucado
(Thomas Nelson).

*"You intended to harm me, but God intended it for good
to accomplish what is now being done, the saving of many lives"*

Genesis 50:20

"'For I know the plans I have for you,' declares the Lord.
"plans to prosper you and not to harm you, plans to give you
hope and a future."

Jeremiah 29:11

Statistics and Resources

Included with my story are several real-life case study scenarios. The system failed me and my siblings, and sadly it's still happening today. Many children are left too long in the system due to the lack of good foster homes or enough families willing to adopt. Furthermore, with the lack of support, many foster families decide not to continue fostering after about one year. Foster care reform has now become a high priority throughout our nation.

Here are some current statistics from Fostering the Family.

430,000 – There are 430,000 children are in foster care throughout our nation and only 214,421 foster parents.

4,500 – There are over 4,500 children in foster care in South Carolina, and 400 of these children are available for adoption.

60% - of children in foster care are between the ages of 0-5 years old.

60% - of children enter foster care because of neglect.

50% - More than 50% of foster parents quit within their first year of service.

65% - An estimated 65% of adoptive placements fail, which results in returning the children to foster care.

2 years – The majority of girls who age out of the system are pregnant within two years.

60% - Over 60% of children caught up in sex trafficking come out of the foster care system.

50% - More than 50% of prison inmates come from the foster system.

With hard work and diligence, change is attainable. I believe now is the time for us to step up and be advocates for all foster care children and to assure their safety. We must do everything humanly possible to keep them safe, give them hope, and be there for them as they search for meaning and purpose in their lives.

If you would like to be involved with this God-sized task, here are some agencies diligently working for change:

Fostering the Family ignites churches and communities to support foster, adoptive and kinship families. They believe a family is the best way to see sustainable change in our society and communities – ultimately making a lasting difference in the life of a vulnerable child. fosteringthefamily.org

PS I Love You Ministries supports the needs of children in foster care and the families who serve them. They provide a cost-free resource center to help meet the physical needs of foster children. Foster families visit their clothing closet at the arrival of a new placement, season change, or after a growth spurt of their current foster children. They give away more than 40,000 items to children in foster care. psiloveyouministries.com

Children's Trust of South Carolina is taking a leadership role in preventing child abuse, neglect, and injury. scchildren.org

Foster Love, formerly Together We Rise is an organization comprised of motivated young adults and former foster youth. They partner with individuals, companies, and community partners to bring resources to foster youth. Their foundation helps to provide thousands of foster youths across the country with new bicycles, college supplies, and duffle bags, known as sweet cases, to children in foster care so they don't have to move from house to house with their belongings in a trash bag. fosterlove.com

Apendix: Case Studies & Letters

The following are actual case study scenarios from anonymous Guardians ad Litem (GAL) and foster mothers. These are only a few cases that happened within the last ten years to current day. I share them with you to show how little progress has been made for improvements in a failing system for both foster care and adoption. The same issues that plagued the system back in 1956, when the four of us were separated, are still issues that need changing today. Until the statutes are corrected, and primary focus is on children, they will continue to fall through the proverbial cracks of a broken system.

While there are many sad stories to share, there are happy ones too. In addition to the case studies, I've included letters from children illustrating their lives in trauma and transition. A caseworker demonstrates the difference we can make in the life of a child in need by opening our homes and hearts and providing unconditional love and care. Allie's story shows that there is hope. Let's do everything possible to make these happy endings more prevalent than the sad ones.

Billy

O ne memorable case was Billy. This one stole my heart, and I became more involved with him than any other case in my nearly forty years as a GAL. Billy, at eight years of age, was the oldest of four children and came from a horrible home situation. This was the worst of all my cases. He had been beaten terribly. The home had no running water, no electricity, no food, and was infested with bugs. The children were begging neighbors for food and living in the woods most of the time, while the parents were doing drugs.

Billy was moved to several therapeutic foster homes as he had many disabilities due to the extreme abuse he suffered. When they could no longer find a suitable therapeutic foster home for Billy, he was moved to a group home about seventy-five miles away. We visited him there several times, and when I found out he had never had a real birthday party, we gave him one for his fifteenth birthday. I will never forget the smiles and hugs we got from him.

When he aged out of the system, I was taken off the case and was told that they were going to find him a group apartment for adults. I lost contact with him after that, but often prayed for him and wondered what happened to him.

Jeffrey

I will never forget my very first case as a GAL. I was new to the whole foster care system and was given a case of a one-year-old child who was taken into custody by DSS. Jeffrey was in and out of the hospital over forty-five times in his very short life with one mysterious illness after another. When he would arrive at the ER, his mother told medical personnel how she had "saved him" by some heroic method from choking or seizures, or that he had been throwing up violently, or some other situation. There never was any medical evidence of anything wrong with Jeffrey. This went on until someone at the ER alerted DSS that they may have a situation with the mother, not the child. When Jeffrey was put in a foster home, the visits to the ER immediately stopped and he appeared to be a happy, healthy child.

Upon doing a lot of research, I came to the conclusion that Jeffrey's mother had a very rare condition called Munchausen syndrome by proxy. This is a mental illness whereby the caretaker of a child, most often a mother, either makes up fake symptoms or causes real symptoms to make it look like the child is sick. They do this in order to make themselves out to be the "heroine" or rescuer. It is a form of child abuse. Jeffrey was in the foster home only a few short months and then returned to his mother. I was concerned because this mental illness cannot be cured in a couple of months and was most certain to happen again. A few months after being returned to his mother, I received a report that Jeffrey was dead. I will never forget the picture of this precious child in his coffin.

Sarah

A s a jail chaplain, I got a case involving a three-year-old minor child by the name of Sarah. I met her mother in jail through my ministry there, and when I found out her child was in custody of DSS, I requested the case since I was authorized to go into the jail already. Sarah's mother, Dixie, was very remorseful over what had happened. In fact, I have never seen a parent so remorseful in my cases.

Dixie was a young single mother who had become addicted to drugs. She had been on drugs since her early teens. She was living in a trailer park with another woman, on a very busy highway in our town. One day, Dixie was passed out on her sofa, and Sarah wandered outside and made her way to the busy highway. A concerned motorist stopped and called the police.

Sarah was placed in an excellent foster home. The couple had two biological children approximately the same age as Sarah. She thrived in this home and was very loved and cared for.

Sarah's father was also in jail over a domestic abuse case with Dixie. He was a very violent man, and it is believed that he abused Sarah as well.

When Sarah's mother got out of jail, she moved out of town to the beach. Instead of staying locally and working on getting her child back, she chose to do her own thing. Sarah stayed in the foster home for several years and did very well there. Dixie kept making excuses about why she couldn't do the required minimum to get her child back, got pregnant, and just gave up. Her parental rights were eventually terminated.

Missy

Missy was six years old when she was taken into protective custody and placed in a foster home. When it was reported, Missy was living in a home with deplorable conditions and numerous health and safety hazards. She was living there with her grandmother and her great-grandfather, who was ninety years old. This was an extremely run-down trailer and half of it had been cut off. An adult protective services order was also received regarding the great-grandfather. When they came to investigate this, they found a horrible situation. The refrigerator had black mold as well as old dishes stacked inside the sink and black mold all over the kitchen floor and walls.

The grandmother appeared to be under the influence of drugs. She refused to participate in a drug screen by hospital staff, and Missy, tested positive for amphetamines. The case was indicated for physical abuse.

Missy was placed in a fantastic foster home where the foster parents had a child the same age as Missy. The girls became very close friends. These parents were Christians and had a lovely home. They were excellent foster parents, and Missy loved living there. She continued to visit regularly with her grandmother while there.

After the grandmother did the required minimum services, Missy was returned to her. Though the grandmother has had an ongoing alcohol and drug problem for many years, DSS never did a random drug test on her. The home situation was not much improved, and Missy and her grandmother moved around from one place to another, wherever they could find someone who would let them stay.

Child Update

Authorities are called to a house where adults are openly using methamphetamines. A male, on the run from the authorities, lives in the home and is using drugs in the presence of children. The home has numerous large dogs and is filthy with feces on the floors.

Neighbors report multiple men coming and going from the house. They expressed their concerns for the child's safety. The child is taken into protective care.

Current status of case:

Mother not enrolled in any services.

Mother visits child twice a month.

Mother ordered to obtain and maintain suitable housing and employment.

Mother must submit to random drug screens.

Mother must attend and complete parenting classes.

Paternity of male unknown; paternity test ordered.

The child has adjusted well to foster care. No adjustment issues to being in foster care and has bonded well with foster family.

The mother has refused to complete the treatment plan. Initial concerns for the child's safety are still present.

Siblings

Two children, a girl aged five and a seven-year-old boy, are removed from a home into emergency care due to a domestic abuse call to Department of Social Services. The father and mother were arguing over a drug deal gone bad.

The five-year-old was found outside the home late at night during cold weather, wearing only underwear. A concerned neighbor called police after hearing screams and finding the child in the yard. Both parents were arrested for domestic abuse. The children were taken into protective custody.

The biological mother has not attended required anger management classes nor attended Alcoholics Anonymous meetings as required by court order. The biological father is still in jail. There is no kinship care available for these children.

The boy and girl are in foster care together. After some initial trauma, both are adjusting well to foster care at this time. The boy has begun school and is in line with most learning abilities; however, he is receiving some remedial classes to catch up on reading skills. The girl is adjusting to a new home environment, but has reverted to occasional bed-wetting.

The foster parents are working with a psychiatrist to address her fears. Both foster children cry nightly, asking why they can't return home. Foster mother believes this will reduce in time. Foster family has two biological children close to same ages and these two foster children are bonding with them.

The case worker is disappointed that the biological mother will not attend her required meetings. She's had more than eight months to prove her desire to get her children back but doesn't seem interested in complying with the court order. She has refused to attend any visitation with her children and refused to show up for mandatory drug testing.

This mother has four more months to attend classes. If she does not comply, and father shows no interest, a plan for permanency will be presented to the judge for TPR. (Termination of Parental Rights). The father has no contact, nor is he showing any interest in his children.

Foster parents were interested in adoption of these two children and waited months for a final hearing to be scheduled by the court. This case had been continued twice, once due to the GAL unable to attend, and once for the case worker requesting continuance due to illness.

The following letters are provided by Plummer Youth Promise and represent children and workers in the foster care system.

It's hard for me to say that I know my foster parents love me. Those words don't come easy to me. But I know it when I see it. So, here are some ways that I see that my foster parents love me.

They respect my privacy. When I tell them something personal, I know that they won't blab it around. Sometimes they have to talk with my social worker and teachers about me. But other than that, they don't go sharing my information with just anyone. That makes it a little easier for me to trust them.

They try to give me choices. I hate it when I have no say in what happens to me because that has happened a lot in my life. When they can, they let me make my own decisions. Even if it's just for a small thing, like letting me decide when I do my homework, I like that they give me some control over my life.

They treat me like a regular kid. I know they try hard to not make me feel different. They treat me just like their other kids. And they make sure I get to do normal stuff like hang out with my friends. I know from experience that sometimes foster kids don't get to do regular stuff because there are all these crazy rules. But my foster parents try hard to make sure the rules don't keep me from doing things that are important to me.

They help me stay in touch with my parents and my brother and sisters. I know it's a hassle sometimes, but they do make sure that I get chances to see my mom even though it means they have to drive me around a lot. Sometimes my brother and sister can come to my house which I really like a lot.

They are really clear that I will stay here until I can go to a permanent family. They can get mad at me sometimes, but they never threaten me with having to leave when I screw up. Sometimes that's the very worst thing about foster care… having to move to another foster home because you messed up or something. I'm pretty sure that won't happen here.

So, like I said, I'm not big on using the L word. But it seems to me that they must love me because of how they take care of me. Not that I am always happy here! But it's good to know that I matter to them. Maybe I love them too, but I'm not ready to say that yet.

Child in foster care

CASE STUDY

Dear Foster Parent,

We work together to help kids in the child welfare system. Usually, we have a cooperative relationship, each doing their part to help a child. We've hit some bumps in the road but managed to work things out between us. I'm not sure you know how much you are valued and loved by those social workers you've come to know.

We love your willingness to welcome a child into your home even when you are asked to do so on short notice. Your flexibility has provided a child with a safe, warm bed when they needed it most, even when it inconvenienced you.

We love the lengths you go to in order to help foster children maintain ties to their families. It takes time and energy to get kids to and from visits with family. You help prepare them for those visits and comfort them when they fall through. You also are there when kids come back from a visit very sad or angry. You get that their feelings aren't about you although you are the one who has to help them manage those intense emotions. And, you do everything possible to help your foster child avoid the loyalty conflicts that plague so many children in care.

We love the unique perspective you have of your foster child. You know them in a way that we can't. You are there for the early morning routines and late-night struggles. You are witness to their finding their place within your family. You see them when they are most vulnerable. Sometimes we forget how valuable your perspective is. Please remind us when we do so because your voice must be heard if we are to do right by kids in care.

We love your ability to fall in love with a foster child. You are the person who loves the challenge of a snarky thirteen-year-old girl who is mad at everyone. Or the foster parent who can care for a young child with complex medical needs no matter how many medical appointments are involved. Or the person willing to provide a loving home for a youth who has moved through multiple foster homes and group homes and has pretty much given up on ever being part of a family. And, who is determined to fight you every step of the way.

We love and respect that your caring for a child includes being able to let them go. Even when it breaks your heart. When a child leaves you to return home to family or to join their adoptive family you are able to celebrate with them despite your own pain. And that, of course, is the ultimate love.....the ability to put someone else's needs before your own.

We love you for so many other things. Even when we forget to acknowledge your contributions please know that you are deeply appreciated and loved by your child welfare partners.

from a social worker

Allie's Story

I was born on a warm June morning. But unlike so many babies who are immediately held and loved by mamas, daddies too—little ones whose parents begin dreaming dreams for them--I came into the world sick. I was addicted to methadone, to be precise—the result of my biological mom's personal drug addiction prior to and during pregnancy.

I, of course, have no memory of this—only some remaining issues that are likely the result of these circumstances. ADD, for example, and that persistent sneezing thing I do when first waking up each morning.

When they released me from the hospital, I was cared for by a guardian. A family friend, she brought me to the social worker who oversaw my case. Guess you could say this person cared for me too—made sure I saw the right doctors and received the best withdrawl treatments. And it's true. I did have to go through withdrawal, which—as the social worker's records state—wasn't always pretty. I ran a fever, coughed and sneezed a lot, not to mention having diarrhea. And boy was I irritable! The records say I fussed and fussed, all through the night sometimes.

Still, I don't blame my birth mom. I know she tried. But kicking a drug habit's a difficult thing, and both her and my birth father hoped they'd get their lives cleaned up so they could bring me home. Be my mom and dad.

That never happened. Instead, my maternal grandfather became my guardian. He and his girlfriend, a wonderful woman I called Bunny, became my parents—eventually adopting me when I was only two.

I suppose they expected to see me through until I graduated from high school. On a bright spring day, however, all that changed when my papa suffered a severe heart attack at the breakfast table. There I sat in my highchair, eating my Cheerios.

All I remember was the loud siren, the rush of men and women whisking Papa away on a stretcher. And I never saw him again.

Bunny? She was sad, I know, but she still had me and, at first, that seemed enough. Unfortunately, the ugly reality of Alzheimer's was taking its toll, and I couldn't stay with her either. I think that made her the most sad—losing me.

Thankfully, my uncle found a great organization that worked hard to place children in loving homes to prevent them from going into foster care. Only a month after my papa's passing, I visited a family in North Carolina. They had a farm and dogs. I love dogs! Oh, and they had extended loving family members who were excited about my visit too—especially a little girl just my age. We were fast friends.

My mom and dad love to say, "She arrived on a bright spring Saturday, suitcase in hand, and she never left."

I journeyed a long, winding road before I'd even turned three, but it brought me to my forever family, and for that, I'm eternally grateful. I'm a believer in happily-ever-afters, even if they come through difficult means, in painful ways. Because God loves to work things out for those who love Him and are called according to His purposes (Romans 8:28).

I'm living proof!

Endorsers

Starr Ayers, author, *For the Love of Emma*, and *Emma's Quest*, and *Room at the Table*.

Christa T. Bell, Attorney, Assistant Solicitor, Kershaw County Solicitor's Office, Camden, SC.

Ali Bragdon, CEO, Oasis of Hope, foster parent

Jessica Brodie, author, speaker, journalist, blogger, and editor of the *South Carolina United Methodist Advocate*; owner/operator of Brodie Media, Lexington, SC.

Susie Boyle, Director of Outreach and Partnerships at Fostering the Family, Tega Cay, SC.

Haley Glover Bryant, of Haley Brant Designs, Website and Social Media Management, photographer, Lexington, SC.

Regina Calcaterra, author, *Etched in Sand*; co-author of *Girl Unbroken*; speaker; co-founding partner in Calcaterra Pollack, LLP law firm, NY.

Lisa Corduan, author, landscape photographer, Lexington, SC.

Tracy Crump, author, freelance editor, speaker; course instructor, Serious Writer; Contributor, *Chicken Soup for the Soul*; co-director at Write Life Workshops. *Guideposts* contributing author, Memphis, TN.

Cortney Donelson, author; owner of vocem, LLC, associate publisher, founder & EIC of *GirlStory Magazine*; acquisitions editor, Morgan James Publishing, Huntersville, NC.

Jeanette Galloway, cousin, former book club leader, Third Monday Book Club, Union, SC, now living in Hartsville, SC.

Laura Spencer Greer, writer, speaker, wellness coach, Christian Writers Fellowship, Long's Chapel, Waynesville, NC.

Lori Hatcher, author, writers' conference speaker; and co-president of Lexington, SC Word Weavers.

Jane Jenkins Herlong, author, *Southern Sass with Sweet Tea Wisdom*, former Miss South Carolina.

Jonathan and Lacey Hines, foster/adoptive parents and advocates, Columbia, SC.

Chip Huggins, retired member of SC House of Representatives, Lexington, SC.

Teresa Janzen, author, speaker, podcast host and publisher, Abundance Books, LLC.

Bethany Jett, author, speaker; marketing strategist; ghostwriter; and co-founder of Serious Writer, Inc., and Platinum Literary Services, Inc.

Joann King, retired director of Bethany Christian Services, a national and international adoption and counseling agency.

Kay Kirby, Director of PS I Love You Ministries, Spartanburg, SC.

Denise Kelso Loock, freelance writer and editor. Founder, Dig Deeper Devotions. Director, Christian Writers Fellowship, Long's Chapel, Waynesville, NC.

Andrea Simmons Merrell, professional freelance editor; finalist for the 2016 Editor of the Year Award Blue Ridge Mountains Christian Writers Conference; and author of many books.

Carolyn McNeill, Guardian Ad Litem, Lexington, SC.

Maureen Miller, author, speaker, storyteller, contributing author at *The Mountaineer* newspaper; Contributing author at Guideposts; Blogger at Inspire a Fire; Waynesville, NC.

Brenda Parks, Vice-President of Children Ministries, Miracle Hill Ministries, Greenville, SC.

Holly G. Pisarik, Attorney, Pisarik Law Firm, Fort Mill, SC; Senior VP of Advocacy and Policy Counsel at SCMA, Columbia, SC

Debbie M. Presnell, writer, speaker, founder of Shine Camp. Author, Shining Through James, Bible Study, Black Mountain, NC.

Mitch Prosser, Interim President, Palmetto Family Council, Columbia, SC.

Maggie Wallem Rowe, speaker, dramatist, author, *This Life We Share*, and *Life is Sweet, Y'all*, Waynesville, NC.

Melanie Shull, founder and editor-in-chief of *Living Real Magazine*; author of *Unlocked Hearts, Unleashed Joy, Forgiveness is Key*; and more.

Cindy Sproles, Speaker, Conference Teacher and author of *What Mama Left Behind, Mercy's Rain, Liar's Winter, and New Sheets; He Said, She Said* devotional; and many more Kingsport, TN.

Ron Tant, former assistant pastor, student pastor, and children's pastor in NC, GA, and AR; state director of Child Evangelism Fellowship of GA, and as VP, CEF Int'l.

Kim Trainer, CEO/Co-Founder, Fostering the Family, Lake Wylie, SC.

Amanda M. Whittle, Director, SC Child Advocacy Agency, Columbia, SC.

Jean Wilund, author, speaker, co-president of Lexington, SC Word Weavers.

and Many More.

JUL • 59

About the Author

Linda Summerford is an award winning author residing in the mountains of Western, North Carolina with her husband, Richard. While serving on a foster care review board, and a task force in South Carolina, she realized the atrocities she and her siblings endured were still happening today. Linda is working toward legisative reforms in the foster care and adoption systems. She is the president of Word Weavers of Maggie Valley, North Carolina. Learn more and connect with Linda at authorlindasummerford.com

www.ingramcontent.com/pod-product-compliance
Lightning Source LLC
Chambersburg PA
CBHW020443130626
46549CB00001B/286